PEER POWER, Book 1
WORKBOOK
Becoming an Effective Peer Helper
and Conflict Mediator,
Third Edition

Campanion book

For Trainer—Peer Power, Book 1, Strategies
for the Professional Leader,
Third Edition

Judith A. Tindall, Ph.D.

Psychologist, L.P.C., Consultant
Rohen and Associates
Psychological Center
St. Charles, MO

ACCELERATED DEVELOPMENT
A member of the Taylor & Francis Group

PEER POWER, Book 1, WORKBOOK
Becoming an Effective Peer Helper and Conflict Mediator, Third Edition

Technical Development: Virginia Cooper
Delores Kellogg
Cynthia Long
Marguerite Mader
Janet Merchant
Sheila Sheward

ISBN: 1-55959-057-2

For additional information and ordering please contact

ACCELERATED DEVELOPMENT
A member of the Taylor & Francis Group
1900 Frost Road, Suite 101
Bristol, PA 19007-1598
1-800-821-8312

DEDICATION

I would like to dedicate this book to all the people that I have trained in peer helping and communication skills for the last 27 years, in schools, agencies, businesses, hospitals and individual clients. Individuals that have become helpers and who still use the skills in their everyday life have impacted this revision. Some of my original programs existed in the Rockwood and Pattonville Schools in St. Louis County. Since that time, the materials have been utilized in a variety of public and private settings.

I want to thank many people who have offered suggestions since the program was published for national distribution in 1978. Modifications in this third edition are an outgrowth of cooperation from those who have used these materials in various settings. This third edition reflects more recent work related to personality type (Type Community) and my understanding of work with diverse populations.

TABLE OF CONTENT

LIST OF RATING SCALES

LIST OF RATING FLOW SHEETS

CHAPTER 1

INTRODUCTORY COMMENTS TO THE TRAINEE

You are beginning a training program that could change your life for the better in some rather unique ways. You are going to learn how to be of significant help to other people. When you have learned skills taught throughout this training, you also will find that you are helping yourself in exciting and interesting ways.

Skills you will be learning not only will be helpful to you as a peer helper, but also will be of benefit to you as you relate daily to others. When people have a concern, they frequently talk to their peers and then second perhaps to professional counselors. For this reason, the belief is that you can assist your peers as well as professional counselors, provided that you learn some helping skills.

The training you are starting probably is different from anything you have attempted. Through the training program you will learn how to listen, understand, and communicate better—to listen to what others are really saying or feeling, to understand what others really mean, and to feed back what you have heard in ways that will enable others to handle some of the rough spots in their lives. By learning what this training is teaching, you really can be of help to others. An added benefit of your new skills in helping your peers to grow will be that you will understand and help yourself to grow. You will learn information about common problems that people encounter such as stress, drugs and alcohol, and many others. You also will discover that these skills will take you through a process of understanding your own values and becoming aware of your own thinking and feeling processes.

The question you may ask is, "How can I do that?" Well, you will learn how to hear what your friends really are saying when they are expressing their feelings. You also will learn effective ways in which you can respond to what they are telling you—to respond in ways which will help them deal with their problems more effectively. You will learn how to express better your own thoughts and feelings, how to be understood more clearly, and how to reduce the trouble that often comes when you tell someone the way you feel. Another skill you will be learning is how to confront others and still keep good feelings between the two of you. Also you will be learning during the training program ways of helping others learn to solve problems and put those solutions into action. You will find yourself, as a result of your skills, being sought after to help others solve conflicts. You might be asked at home, school, or your work place to help solve those conflicts. The end result is that you will become a natural helper in a variety of situations and hopefully a more caring person. With these basic skills you will be able to do many things as a peer helper. You may want to see people individually, answer the phone in a drop-in center, lead a discussion group, tutor, lead classroom groups, train others in listening skills, be a more effective community volunteer, or perform other people-helping activities.

The total training program is designed to help you become a better friend, helper, and person. You will learn how to relate to others in ways that will create friendships, develop helping skills, and cause you to value yourself more. Ultimately, the program will create a more caring and friendly school, work place and/or community that is focused on helping as opposed to aggression and conflict.

Peer helping training is more than the kind of training in which you sit and listen to a trainer lecture. When each new skill is presented in the training session, the trainer will demonstrate the behavior. After the trainer has demonstrated the skill, you will be asked to practice that skill. The procedure for the training you are about to receive will follow this general pattern. First, the trainer will explain and demonstrate the new skill to be learned. Second, you will become a helper and practice the skill with other trainees acting as helpers and raters. Third, you will receive feedback from the raters as to how well you performed the skill being practiced and learned. This book, *Peer Power, Book 1, Workbook*, contains information and exercises so that you can become prepared and practice the skills.

To learn peer helping skills, you, the trainee, must be involved actively in what is happening. You are encouraged to become involved—involved in the training, involved in doing the activities suggested in this book, and involved with the other trainees who are learning with you. Based upon the experience of others, you will be excited about learning how to relate better and help others more. How much you learn will depend upon you and how much you want to learn. An exciting experience awaits you in the weeks ahead. We wish you the best in the new venture.

CHAPTER 2

OVERVIEW
PEER HELPING
TRAINING PROGRAM

Peer helping has been expanding at a rapid pace in the last few years. Young people and adults of all ages are learning how to better help their peers—people who share related values, experiences, and life-styles and who are comparable in age.

Peer helping is the process of helping another person. That is, an individual enters into a one-to-one helping relationship, group leadership role, discussion leadership role, advisement, tutoring, volunteering in the community, support group leadership role, or some other interpersonal helping role.

Peer helping has been cited as one of the most effective prevention strategies available. The reason for the effectiveness is not just learning helping behaviors, but putting them into action and practicing the skills learned. Examples of typical prevention activities may center around reducing HIV in adults, teen pregnancy rate, conflicts, gang warfare, school dropouts, community problems, and conflicts in the work places. Examples of these programs go by various names, for example in many of your colleges they are called Peer Leaders. In high school sometimes they are called "PALS" for Peer Assistant Leaders. In the middle schools they often go by a variety of names such as "Peer Helpers," "Peer Facilitators," and "Peer Mediators." At the elementary school level they are sometimes called "Peace Makers." In the community they may be called "Neighbors Helping Neighbors." In business and industry they maybe called "Volunteers." Each program has its own unique name.

Peer helping skills have been utilized with individuals and groups as peer helpers attempt intervention to help others develop more positive behaviors. They work with peers to assist them in overcoming unhealthy life-styles such as excessive use of alcohol and drugs, and eating problems. The intervention often leads the person with the problem to getting assistance from a professional. Examples are volunteers in the work place and peer helpers in schools. Peer helping skills also are used with those in conflict. Some people need much support because they are trying to help themselves. Through peer helping, others are supported in the recovery process. Examples of these are Teen Helpers, supporting group leaders, Help Network in higher education and support groups in the geriatric populations.

As we move toward a more global economy, in many areas of the country what were minorities have become the majority. In today's world an important part of living is to know how to relate to others of different cultures. Often vast differences exist among cultures. For example, you may be a member of a given race but depending upon the area in which you are reared, your values, your concepts and your religion may be different from another person of your race who had different childhood experiences.

As you become more aware of the needs of the community you may choose to volunteer in nursing homes, preschool, homeless shelters, hospitals, and other settings. For you to be truly effective in your volunteer helping role you need to first be trained in peer helping skills. The key is the explanation of what needs to be done, obtaining of actual training, and then having the opportunity to process the volunteer experience.

A peer helper refers to a person who assumes the role of a helping person with contemporaries. The term "peer" denotes a person who shares related values, experiences and life-style, and is approximately the same age.

The training program for peer helping will provide the practice you need for learning the skills necessary for becoming a peer helper. The necessary training time varies, generally requiring 16 to 28 hours of training session time in which you interact with the trainer and the other trainees in the program. In addition, you will spend 29 to 46 hours in preparation time so as to utilize the training session time better. You will be assisted throughout the program by a leader who has the know-how to help you learn the necessary skills.

You will have the fun of learning the skills with others of your age. The training program will include not only yourself but others with whom you will interact and share ideas, feelings, and concerns. You will role-play, assuming the role of helper at times, of helpee at times, and, at other times, of some other person needed in the training technique. As rater you will observe helper/helpee communications during practice. You will be able to try skills and to watch others try the same skills. You will receive feedback, that is, information from others (raters) about how they perceive your skills and how you might improve those skills. You, too, will be asked to be a rater, that is, to give constructive feedback to others in your group. The rater will provide feedback as to the quality, accuracy, and effectiveness of the helping responses by the helper. After you receive feedback, the skill can be practiced again for improvement.

Young people and adults of all ages enjoy learning peer helping because the training is done in a manner in which they can practice together and help one another learn. They learn how to respond to feelings, problems, concerns, and other human needs of people they may help in the future but also of their friends and others they meet daily. By completing peer helper training, an individual often learns to understand himself or herself better. Communication skills in everyday living often are improved through the peer helping program.

Through the **POWER** of **PEERS,** a more caring community is created. If we look at the word **POWER,** it can explain the strength of an effective peer helping program in your school/community/workplace.

P......a **peer** is a person who shares related values, experiences, and life-style.

O......**ownership** implies that the peer has developed the helping skills and has some stake in the impact of the peer helping program.

W......the **wealth** of peers means that peers are used as resources to help others.

E......refers to the **empowerment** given to the peer helpers.

R......refers to the **responsibility** given to the peer helper to carry out the peer helping program.

CHAPTER 3

ROLES FOR PEER HELPERS

Peer helpers are functioning effectively in various settings including schools, churches, teen and crisis centers, clubs and community organizations, and other community agencies engaged in helping through interpersonal relationships. In schools peer helpers work with other students in both groups and one-to-one relationships. The peer helper can be a vital assistant to the professional counselor by extending helping services to more students than could be served by the professional counselor alone.

Peer helpers are trained to function in an interpersonal capacity, therefore they should not be used as clerical assistants. The most obvious role for peer helpers is that of one-to-one interpersonal relationship. Talking with others about their personal problems; talking with disruptive students; referring peers to other sources of help in the community; giving information about drugs, sex, and venereal diseases; and helping others with their school and work place problems are types of assistance given by peer helpers on a one-to-one basis.

Peer helpers can be effective in group settings. They can be used as group leaders, assistants to health educators, teachers of interpersonal skills to other students in counseling groups, or communication skills trainers in the classroom. Peer helpers also can confront other peers in areas of alcohol and drug abuse and get them to seek professional help.

Some of the educational functions peer helpers can perform are tutoring students in academic areas, serving as readers for handicapped students, and helping younger students develop academic skills through tutoring.

Peer helpers can assist in many guidance activities. Some of these involve working in an organized manner with new students, employees, members in nursing homes, or serving as special friend. They can be used to help with the registration process in terms of selection of classes or other options available if working in a community agency. They can work with persons in the career center and assist students and others with many of the computer programs now available. They also can help with the guidance newsletter, serve as testing proctors, and work in many other areas.

The need for peer helpers and opportunities available are tremendous in clubs and community organizations or in any setting where interpersonal relationships are essential. Peer helpers training as outlined in this book will enable people of all ages to help not only their peers better but also themselves.

In religious settings, peer helping is meeting vital needs because of increased demand by church members for counseling. Persons who have completed peer helping training are increasing the number of people who are competent in human relationship communication and other interpersonal concerns. Often in church settings small groups of people are formed and individuals can meet in open, informal, face-to-face contact situations characterized by warmth and intimacy. In this setting, the peer helper can make a major contribution. Peer helpers can be used as assistants in religious education similar to their roles in public and private schools. They can participate in outreach programs for nonmembers such as those in drop-in centers.

In crisis centers, drop-in centers, drug treatment centers, and teen centers, peer helpers have major activities which are being handled effectively. The peer helper who has a value system in keeping with the persons using the centers can hear, understand, and have empathy with persons needing help. The peer helper can communicate in a meaningful way with people for whom a center operates as well as better communicate those people's needs to persons employed within those centers. Thus, peer helpers close the gap between professionals and those individuals who do and those individuals who will make use of the centers.

Assistance to the poor is an important role for the peer helper. Services offered within the community often have not been highly successful with the poor. Peer helpers, persons trained in peer helping from among the rank and file of the poor for whom the services are aimed, can make a difference. The peer helper understands their problems, has a comparable value system, talks the language of people involved, and can do much for others.

Peer professionals in a wide variety of settings can make a difference in the personal growth of others. Often Employee Assistance Programs (EAP) have volunteers that serve as peer helpers to confront troubled employees, find help, and offer support after treatment. Paraprofessionals working with youth in restricted settings such as hospitals and prisons have found that these peer helper skills are beneficial in their daily operations.

Peer helpers possessing various kinds of personalities and levels of training are found in many different settings. The following is a partial list:

Examples of Peer Helping in Elementary Schools

—Peer Tutors
—Study Skills Leaders
—Creative Writing Helpers
—Peer Listeners
—Physical Education Pals
—Creative Dramatics Helpers
—Computer Tutors
—Small Group Discussion Leaders
—Peer Editing Group Leaders
—Conflict Mediators
—Summer Camp Helpers
—Science Helpers
—Art Helpers
—Game Day Players
—Special Friends
—Playground Helpers
—Homework Organizers

In Elementary School Classrooms

—Peer Editing Group Leaders
—Study Circle Helpers
—Cooperative Learning Teachers/Leaders
—Reading Pairs
—Physical Education Helpers
—Music, Art, or Drama Day Helpers
—Bulletin Board Visual Assistants
—Lesson Review Leaders
—Individual Tutors
—Mathematical Helpers
—Spelling Practice Helpers
—Science Lab Assistants
—Phonics Drills Assistants
—Listening Skills Trainers
—Vocabulary Activity Leaders

In Middle Schools

—Peer Tutors
—Peer Facilitators
—Student Buddies
—Advisors
—Big Brothers/Big Sisters
—PTA Helpers
—Peer Listeners
—Conflict Mediators

—Big and Small Group Discussion Leaders
—Peer Problem Topics Leader
—Tutors
—Orientation Helpers
—Homework Helpers
—Classroom Topic Leaders
—Special Days Coordinators
—Special Friends
—Volunteers

In High Schools

—Peer Tutors
—Big Brothers/Big Sisters
—Peer Resource Center Helpers
—Group Leaders
—Peer Drama Assistants
—Orientation Helpers
—Special Topic Seminar Leaders
—Study Buddies
—Conflict Resolution Group Leaders
—Peer Program Trainers
—Peer Facilitators
—In-school Suspension Group Leaders
—Guidance and Students Services Assistants
—New Student Buddies
—Peer Listeners
—Freshmen Support Team Assistants
—Special Day Sponsors
—Crisis Support Group Leaders
—Field Day Helpers
—Resource Centers Assistants
—College Prep Advisors
—Community Service Projects Assistants
—Leaders

In Higher Education

—Hot Line Service Answerers
—Peer Helpers/Peer Tutors
—Drama Day Assistants
—Special Friends to Foreign Students
—Recruitment Assistants
—Freshmen Orientation Helpers
—Resident Hall Advisors
—Career Center Assistants
—Conflict Mediators
—Support Group Leaders
—Classroom Discussion Leader on Special Health Topics
—Health Educators
—Community Service Workers

In The Community

-Peer Hotline Answerers
-Dial Homework Helpers
-Crisis Intervention Helpers
-Recreation Department Helpers
-Business Interns
-Meals On Wheels Assistants
-Conflict Resolution Peer Helpers
-Parenting Helpers
-After School Care Helpers
-Adopt a Grandparent Helpers
-Humane Society Helpers
-Hospital Helpers
-Youth Coordinators
-Peer Ministry Assistants
-4-H Programs Assistants
-Cultural Art Helpers
-Retirement Homes Peer Helpers
-Support Group Leaders
-Pregnancy Prevention Peer Helpers
-Health Education Assistants
-Helpers for the Homeless

In The Workplace

Certain Health Topic Discussers
Peer Helpers with Given Departments or Work Units
One-on-one Helpers
Support Group Leaders

A commitment which you as a trainee in peer helping must consider is whether or not you will strive to learn the interpersonal skills that will enable you to help your peers. If you commit yourself, the trainer in the program will help you learn the necessary skills.

The next challenge which you as a trainee need to consider is whether or not you will be willing to accept new challenges that you may have as a result of becoming a peer helper. You probably will improve your social position among your peers because you will be better able to help them. Thus, you will be expected to assume new responsibilities among your peers—a new role, one which can add new dimensions to your life.

Unit **A**

SETTING
THE
STAGE

SETTING THE STAGE

Before you can begin to learn specific helping skills, it is important for you to understand helping, your reason for wanting to learn helping skills, and what kind of role you would like to have once you are trained. Participating in Module I activities will assist you. For you to truly feel a part of your peer helping program, this unit is important for you to get oriented to the whole concept of peer helping.

For you to be an effective helper to others, you need to understand yourself and how you relate to others. Module II will assist you as you learn more about yourself and the world you live in.

Module III will assist you in looking at the world of helping. Most of you have been a helper in your family, neighborhood, school, and work. Many of you have been helped by someone else. Some things you do are helpful to others and some things are not. Some things we do create dependency on us rather that people learning to take care of themselves. Module III will help you focus on your helper as well as how you currently help others.

Many of you may be using some bad habits that actually inhibit or stop communications. Module IV will help you recognize communication stoppers that close down communication.

Unit A will help you set the stage for developing helping skills in you. Unit A sometime is done at a retreat setting or in a class. At the end of SETTING THE STAGE, my hope is that you will know other trainees very well.

> *"To do good things in the world, first*
> *You must know who you are and what*
> *Gives meaning in your life."*
>
> *Paula P. Brownlee*

MODULE I

What Is Peer Helping?

WHAT IS PEER HELPING?

Since this is our first session together, let's gain an understanding of what each person in the group knows about peer helping. Training then can be slanted for each of you to accomplish your goals. During the first session, you and the trainer during the first session can discuss the structure of the training program, what kinds of things you will be learning, and what you can do after you complete the program.

Peer helping, working with others, is based on communication. Some communication techniques are natural and are used regularly in one's everyday association with others. Before starting training, you need to identify what you already do that contributes to peer helping action and to identify what may need to be learned or improved that will make you an effective peer helper.

This module consists of six exercises in which you will do the following:

1. The first exercise is termed "Pretest" which properly should be called a "self test." The purpose of the exercise is for you to assemble and analyze your knowledge in communicating effectively as a helping person.

2. The second exercise is designed to help you look at common problems within your setting.

3. The third exercise centers on the kind of helping role that you hope to have after training.

4. The fourth exercise is your reason for training.

5. The fifth activity will help establish your norms for training.

6. The sixth exercise involves your contract for training.

Use: In some of exercises in this module wording is supplied so as to be most appropriate for your age. For example, two pretests are supplied: one for youth and the other for adults.

Exercise 1.1

Name _____

Date _____ Hour _____

PRETESTING YOURSELF
COMMUNICATIONS EXERCISE

A helpful person is one who is getting along with himself/herself and who is genuine (not phony) when talking with others. When talking with other people, a helpful person is understanding of and respects the feelings of others. A helpful person seems very confident and all actions are very natural. A helpful person easily can make adjustments to many different kinds of people and still be capable of letting individuals know his/her feelings at the right time.

GOAL

In this exercise you will assess your current level of listening skills

DIRECTIONS FOR STATEMENTS 1 THROUGH 5

1. Wait until the trainer instructs you to complete the material in Module I. The following pages contain five statements which you are to assume are made to you by other persons.

2. Rate each of the four responses given to the statement in order of the response's helpfulness. A rating of Low (L) means no help, a rating of Medium (M) means some help, and a rating of High (H) means a high degree of help.

RATING SCALE FOR RESPONSES

High (H):   The response is extremely helpful and meets all the conditions described in a helpful response.

Medium (M):   The response is of some help to another person.

Low (L):   The response is not helpful to another person.

EXERCISE FOR YOUTH
(For Adult use, see statements 1B through 10B following.)

Statement 1A:

"My parents won't let me go over there at night. They say that I'll get into trouble if I hang around with those kids."

Responses for Statement 1A:

__1a. What have you done that makes your parents not trust you?

__1b. What they don't know won't hurt them. Your mistake is telling them too much about what you do.

__1c. It's hard sometimes to accept your parents' ideas on things.

__1d. It is upsetting because your parents won't let you be with the kids. It's like they don't trust your judgment.

Statement 2A:

"Those snobs won't ask me. . .they think they are better than me. . .who needs 'em, anyhow?"

Responses for Statement 2A:

__2a. Why don't you stop pouting about it and find somebody else?

__2b. It makes you mad to think that others think you're not good enough to be with them.

__2c. You'd like to be involved with them but they show no interest, it really makes you wonder about what to do.

__2d. That's the approach I take with stuck-up people. . .just get as far away as I can.

Statement 3A:

"My grades are horrible. My parents have grounded me for a month, and I've lost my allowance. I don't know what else could go wrong."

Responses for Statement 3A:

__3a. This predicament has you feeling so low it makes you wonder if anything else could go wrong.

__3b. Don't worry, there's always something worse to come along.

__3c. I know what you mean. I've had that same thing happen to me. You feel just like everything is sour at once.

__3d. Quit feeling sorry for yourself. It won't help a lot.

Statement 4A:

"I try so hard to be good in P.E. but I get so embarrassed because I can't play football.

Responses for Statement 4A:

__4a. Sometimes you just have to face the idea that you can't be good in football.

__4b. Sometimes it's hard to feel good about playing football even though you do your best.

__4c. Why don't you try to get out of P.E.?

__4d. What have you done to learn to play football?

Statement 5A:

"I have some new friends that my parents don't like because of their long hair, but my parents really don't know them."

Responses for Statement 5A:

__5a. What have you done that makes your parents not like your friends?

__5b. Why don't you go along with your parents and find different friends?

__5c. It makes you feel that your parents don't trust you to choose new friends.

__5d. You should go ahead and be friends anyway.

Statement 6A:

"I have a sister who can't keep her mouth shut. No matter what I tell her, she tells everyone."

Write what you would say in response: _____

_____

Statement 7A:

"I really hate school. It seems like there is nothing that I like about it anymore, and I am just stuck."

Write what you should say in response: _____

_____

Statement 8A:

"It is a real hassle going here everyday. There is always pressure to do things their way."

Write what you would say in response: _____

_____

Statement 9A:

"My brothers are driving me crazy. They are always in trouble. It is hard being kin to them."

Write what you would say in response: _____

_____

Statement 10A:

"I just found out that I am going to have to have an operation. I do not like hospitals, doctors, and nurses. I don't like needles either."

Write what you would say in response: _____

_____

EXERCISE FOR ADULTS

Statement 1B:

"My boss is giving me a hard time. No matter how much I do, he always finds something else that I need to do."

Responses for Statement 1B:

__1a. What have you done that always makes your boss find additional things for you to do.

__1b. What your boss thinks is not important. Just tell him to buzz off.

__1c. It's hard at times to accept feedback from your boss.

__1d. It is frustrating that you work so hard, and your boss gives you a hard time.

Statement 2B:

"I am new here and I am so lonely. I am afraid to make friends because I always get hurt."

Responses for Statement 2B:

___2a. Why don't you just make friends anyway?

___2b. Here you run from people, and you don't have friends.

___2c. You feel really lonely because you don't have friends even though you are afraid to reach out because you might get hurt.

Statement 3B:

"I just lost my job, I had an automobile accident that totaled my car. I don't know what else could go wrong."

Responses to Statement 3B:

___3a. Quit feeling sorry for yourself. It won't help a lot.

___3b. You are really feeling down because you just lost both your job and your transportation.

___3c. Things seem like everything is wrong.

Statement 4B:

"I try so hard to lose weight, but no matter what I do, I can't keep it off."

Responses to Statement 4B:

___4a. Just quit trying and accept yourself.

___4b. You would like to lose weight.

___4c. You feel discouraged because no matter what you do to lose weight, you can't.

Statement 5B:

"I don't like the kids that my son is hanging around with. They are always in trouble."

Responses to Statement 5B:

___5a. Just tell him that he can't hang around them.

___5b. What kind of trouble are they in?

___5c. You are concerned about the kids your son hangs around with because they are always in trouble.

Statement 6B:

"I have a coworker who can't keep her mouth shut. No matter what I tell her, she tells everyone."

Write what you would say in response: _____

_____

Statement 7B:

"I really hate my job. It seems like there is nothing that I like about it anymore, and I am just stuck."

Write what you would say in response: _____

_____

Statement 8B:

"It is a real hassle going to work everyday. There is always pressure to get things done."

Write what you would say in response: _____

_____

Statement 9B:

"My kids are driving me crazy. They are always in trouble. It is hard being a single parent."

Write what would you say in response: _____

_____

Statement 10B:

"I just found out that I am going to have to have an operation. I do not like being in hospitals. I don't like needles either."

Write what you would say in response: _____

_____

Exercise 1.2

Name _____

Date _____ Hour _____

PROBLEMS, PROBLEMS, PROBLEMS

GOAL

In this exercise you will become aware of problems which are faced by people at school, at work, or within the community.

DIRECTIONS

1. Look at the two lists of problems supplied in this exercise and select the list most appropriate for your age.

2. Add additional problems if you know some.

3. Of the problems listed, check the ones that you believe are important.

4. Rank in order those problems which you believe are the most pressing problems for people your age. Use 1 for the most important, 2 for next most, etc.

5. Share your top three rankings with others and your reasons for placing them as the top three.

6. Compare the list with others and try to move toward an agreement within your group.

7. List the top three problems your training group have identified.

8. Summarize from your listing of problems and sharing of ideas with your peers what you think about kinds of problems most people have.

YOUTH LIST

Check if Important	Problem	Rank Order
_____	Academic Failure	_____
_____	Fear	_____
_____	Poor Relationships with Friends	_____
_____	Poor Relationships with Parents	_____
_____	Drug and/or Alcohol Use	_____
_____	Cigarette Use	_____

_____	Gangs	_____
_____	Racial Relations	_____
_____	Feeling Isolated	_____
_____	Lack of Confidence	_____
_____	Peer Pressure	_____
	Others (List)	
_____	_____	_____
_____	_____	_____
_____	_____	_____

ADULT LIST

Check if important	Problem	Rank order
_____	Lack of Work Skills	_____
_____	Poor Relationship with Coworkers	_____
_____	Poor Relationship with Family	_____
_____	Health Problems	_____
_____	Anxiety	_____
_____	Depression	_____
_____	Career Change	_____
_____	Conflicts at Work	_____
_____	Alcohol Abuse	_____
_____	Other Drug Abuse	_____
	Others (List)	
_____	_____	_____
_____	_____	_____
_____	_____	_____

HOMEWORK

Study Exercise 1.3 and complete it before the next group meeting.

Exercise 1.3

MY PEER HELPING ROLE

GOAL

In this exercise you will identify potential roles in which you may serve as a peer helper.

DIRECTIONS

1. Look at the peer helper lists provided in Chapter 3 and check one or more roles that you would like to perform as a peer helper.

2. Identify your natural skills and attitudes that would help you with these roles. Three examples are provided. Add your list using your skills, a possible peer helper role, and a potential setting.

Skills		My skills
Ex:	Friendliness	List: _____
	Math Ability	_____
	Acting Ability	_____

Role		My peer helping role
Ex:	Peer Problem Discusser	List: _____
	Mathematic Tutor	_____
	Theater Assistant	_____

Setting		Where I will help
Ex:	Community	List: _____
	School	_____
	Church	_____
	Workplace	_____

HOMEWORK

Study Exercise 1.4 and complete it before the next group meeting.

Name _____

Date _____ Hour _____

YOUR REASON FOR TRAINING

GOAL

In this exercise you will be able to examine your personal reasons for learning peer helping skills.

DIRECTIONS

1. Please write your responses to the three questions.

2. Discuss your responses with your training group.

3. Turn the sheet into your trainer when the exercise is completed.

QUESTIONS

1. In what type of situations do you plan to use skills in communications and leadership

   training? _____

   _____

   _____

2. How could the skills fit into your personal life? _____

   _____

   _____

3. What reasons did you have for joining this training group? _____

   _____

   _____

HOMEWORK

Study Exercise 1.5 and complete Directions 1 and 2 before the next group meeting.

NORMS FOR TRAINING

INTRODUCTION

In order for you to feel comfortable with your training group, certain norms must be set by the group.

GOAL

In this exercise, you will establish norms for yourself and your training group.

DIRECTIONS

1. Make a list of conditions that are important to you when you are participating in a group. (Example: keeping things discussed private).

    _____

    _____

    _____

2. Make a list of actions that you need from others in the group. (Example: others will listen to you when you talk).

    _____

    _____

    _____

3. Share your lists from Numbers 1 and 2 with your group leader and other group members.

4. Discuss as a group what norms you will establish.

5. Write the list of norms on which your group has decided.

    _____

    _____

    _____

HOMEWORK

Study Exercise 1.6 and complete it before the next group meeting.

Exercise 1.6

CONTRACT FOR TRAINING

INTRODUCTION

Certain conditions are essential for training. Learning to be peer helpers necessitates good learning conditions.

GOAL

In this exercise you will sign your contract with your trainer.

DIRECTIONS

1. Based on the norms discussed in Exercise 1.5, please list on the sheet entitled "My Contract for Training" those things you agree to do.

2. Share your list with your trainer.

3. If your trainer and you agree upon the list, then both of you sign the contract.

HOMEWORK

Read the Introduction to Module II and complete Directions 1 and 2 in Exercise 2.1 before the next group meeting.

MY CONTRACT FOR TRAINING

I, _____, agree to do the
following during my peer helper training:

1. _____

_____

2. _____

_____

3. _____

_____

4. _____

_____

5. _____

_____

Signed:

Trainee_____ Date _____

Trainer_____ Date _____

MODULE II

Understanding Yourself and Others

UNDERSTANDING YOURSELF AND OTHERS

The initial meetings of the Peer Helping Training Program will help you understand yourself and others in the program. The first step in helping others is understanding yourself. Conflict arises when you don't know yourself or others.

Because you as trainees will be spending much time together for the next several weeks, benefits could be gained by getting to know one another early in the program.

You will have an opportunity to share information about yourself with your training group. You also will have time to learn about others in your group. You will do a variety of exercises that will help you look at your values, identify some of your basic needs, get to know yourself through type, examine your own strengths and growth areas, and understand better others who are different from you.

People who truly understand themselves will improve interpersonal relationships, decrease stress, work more effectively on a team, increase productivity, and go further in understanding others of different cultures.

Understanding people of different cultures is important because of our changing world. The need for tolerance and understanding becomes important as you consider this picture.

If we could shrink the earth's population (5.2 billion) to a village of precisely 1000, with all existing population ratios remaining the same. The resulting numbers would be as follows:

Village of 1,000

Geographical Origin

564 Asians and Oceanians
210 Europeans
86 Africans
80 South Americans
60 North Americans

Skin Color
820 of the 1000 would be nonwhite
180 would be white

Wealth
50% of the entire world's wealth would be in the hands of only 60 people

Literacy
700 would be unable to read

Nutrition
500 would suffer from malnutrition

Housing
600 would live in substandard housing.

(Hodgkinson, 1992)

Some of these exercises will be utilized in the group and others will be utilized by yourself. If you only have a short amount of time, you may want to use only Exercise 2.2.

In this module you as a trainee will serve as a listener and reverse roles to serve as the individual who shares information. Understanding among participants begins with this session.

Use: This entire module can be used with either or both adolescents and/or adults.

Exercise 2.1

Name _____

Date _____ Hour _____

HELPING VALUES

Values are often the basis for how we live our lives; therefore, to know our helping values is very important.

GOAL

In this exercise you will identify your helping values.

DIRECTIONS

1. Look at the list, on the next page, of possible values and add additional values that are important to you.

Values	Rank Order
Family	_____
Friends	_____
Advancement	_____
Spirituality	_____
Meaningful Work	_____
Helping Others	_____
Having Fun	_____
Health	_____
Serenity	_____
Others (Please list)	
_____	_____
_____	_____
_____	_____

2. Rank your values in order. (Use 1 for highest rank, 2 for next highest, etc.)

3. Discuss with your group how these values guide you in everyday living.

HOMEWORK

Study and complete Exercise 2.2 before the next group meeting.

Exercise 2.2

Name _____

Date _____ Hour _____

MY NEEDS

GOAL

In this exercise you will understand better your own needs as they apply to peer helping.

DIRECTIONS

1. Read the following information about needs.

Abraham Maslow, a well-know psychologist, developed a theory regarding human needs and motivation that is useful in understanding the motivating factor that affect human behavior and personality. He presented these in a hierarchy of five categories in order of importance. His theory states that one cannot move to a higher need until the lower needs have been satisfied. The following is a list of needs as he presented them.

Physiological Needs

These needs are the lowest form and are directly related to survival and self preservation. Primary survival needs include such things as the need for oxygen, food, water, rest, warmth, exercise, excretion, and avoidance of bodily harm. Maslow believed these needs are so important that a person can do or think of little else until they are satisfactorily met. However, their importance diminishes as they become satisfied or are in a state of equilibrium when the next category of needs in the hierarchy comes into play.

Safety Needs

These needs are related to physical and psychological security and reflect a desire to be safe from personal violence or harm as well as to avoid the unpredictable.

Love Needs

These needs are related to a desire for a sense of belonging and acceptance. Satisfaction involves both opportunities for giving and receiving.

Esteem Needs

These go beyond love needs into a more active desire for recognition and self-esteem. Maslow classified these into two sub-categories: 1) the desire for strength or achievement and 2) the desire for recognition, importance, and appreciation. Satisfaction leads to self-confidence.

Self-actualization Needs

These highest needs come into prominence once all the lower needs are met to a satisfactory degree. These include the need for a person to maximize potential to reach the peak of unique abilities and talents. Creativity, curiosity, ambition, and independence are all related to self-actualization. Unlike the house pet which only strives to be well fed, warm, and cuddled, the human animal strives for much more that often takes forms of expression through creative or competitive efforts in the arts, sciences, athletics, or religious life.

2. Study the hierarchy of needs that follows:

	My Needs	Family's Needs
SELF-ACTUALIZATION NEEDS Uniqueness	_____	_____
ESTEEM NEEDS Self-respect Recognition Self-esteem Statue Prestige Attention	_____ _____ _____ _____ _____ _____	_____ _____ _____ _____ _____ _____
LOVE NEEDS Acceptance Love Friendship Understanding	_____ _____ _____ _____	_____ _____ _____ _____
SAFETY NEEDS Structure Order Security Protection Freedom from fear	_____ _____ _____ _____ _____	_____ _____ _____ _____ _____
PHYSIOLOGICAL NEEDS Food Water Warmth	_____ _____ _____	_____ _____ _____

As lower level needs are met, higher levels come into play.   (Foster, 1992)

LOWEST LEVEL

3. To the right of the needs listed in Item 2, place an "X" beside those needs you think you have.

4. In Item 2, place an "F" beside those needs you think your family has.

5. Identify needs that you expect to be met through your peer helping roles.

HOMEWORK

1. Write a paragraph explaining how peer helping will meet specific needs for you and identify those needs.

2. Study Exercise 2.3 and come prepared to complete it during the next group meeting.

Exercise 2.3

Name _____

Date _____ Hour _____

KNOWING OTHERS

Since we will be spending several hours together, we will benefit by getting to know each other as soon as possible. The following are directions for the group to follow during the introduction game.

GOALS

In this exercise you will learn

1. names of the people in the training group,

2. to develop your listening behaviors, and

3. to understand how to relate to others.

DIRECTIONS

1. Select a partner (someone whom you don't already know or know well). One of you serves as the listener and the other tells about himself/herself. Each one of you talks for about three minutes, sharing information about yourself such as your hobbies, things that you like doing, things that bug you, what you are trying to change in yourself, family information, and so forth. The listener may ask questions at any time. Then change roles so that you serve both as a listener and as the person who is sharing information about himself/herself.

2. After completing activities in Direction 1, introduce your partner. When speaking stand directly behind the person being introduced and place both hands on the other person's shoulders. The person being introduced will remain seated and silent. You may wish to give the introduction in first person form. (i.e., "My name is" rather than "His name is" or "Her name is.") This process will create some interesting awareness with regard to listening skills.

3. After all introductions have been completed, write responses to questions in the exercise or discuss them with the total group.

QUESTIONS

1. How did you feel about being introduced by someone else?

   _____

   _____

2. How did you feel about introducing someone else?

   _____

   _____

3. What did you learn about other group members?

   _____

   _____

4. What did you learn about yourself?

   _____

   _____

5. What are your feelings about the group members?

   _____

   _____

HOMEWORK

1. Complete this exercise and be prepared to submit it to your group leader at the next meeting.

2. Read introduction to Exercise 2.4 and complete as much of it as possible before the next group meeting.

Exercise 2.4

Name _____

Date _____ Hour _____

UNDERSTANDING MYSELF THROUGH TYPE

INTRODUCTION:

Often a person's personality type can influence the way the person feels about self and others. The Myers-Briggs Type Indicator (MBTI) and the Myers-Briggs Type Indicator Expanded Analytic Report (MBTI-EAR) are useful measures of type and can supply information for helping you understand yourself and others. If you understand yourself and others, you will find it easier to relate to your family, friends, and coworkers.

For example, your best friend Bill never wants to make definite plans for the weekend. He always has other options he wants to consider. You on the other hand like to know what your plans are so you can be ready to plan your weekend. You would like to do things with Bill because he is lots of fun; however, until you learned about type, you had a hard time with this behavior.

If you want to take the Myers-Briggs Type Indicator (MBTI), you will need to have a professional counselor or psychologist administer it to you. If you have not yet taken it, you may want to inquire about a local source that can administer it and give you information about your type.

Carl Jung was the first to write about preferences and later Katherine Cook Briggs and Isabel Briggs Myers developed the MBTI to assist others in understanding themselves and others. The idea behind the sixteen types represent the lifelong work of Isable Briggs Myers. In 1962 Educational Testing Service published the Myers-Briggs Type Indicator, a paper and pencil instrument that Isabel developed over a twenty year period with Katherine Briggs, her mother. Regarded as a research instrument, it did not have a wide circulation or usage until Consulting Psychologist Press assumed responsibility for publishing it in 1975. The Indicator was developed specifically to carry Carl Jung's theory of type (June, 1921-71) into practical applications.

They felt a useful way to look at individual differences is by identifying the different psychological types, which is described as follows:

1. The first has to do with where you get your energy—from outside yourself (Extraversion, abbreviated as "E") or from within yourself (Introversion, abbreviated as "I").
   E—"Let's talk about the problem."
   I—"Let's think about the problem."

2. The second has to do with how you gather information about your world—in a literal, sequential way (Sensing, abbreviated by "S") or in a more figurative, random way (Intuition, abbreviated by "N").
   S—"Let's read the directions for doing the game."
   N—"Let's invent our own way of playing the game."

3. The third relates to the way you prefer to make decisions—objectively and impersonally (Thinking, abbreviated by "T") or interpersonally (Feeling, abbreviated by "F").

    T—"I think it is a good idea because it is the best price."
    F—"I feel it is a good idea because others will enjoy it."

4. The last has to do with your day-to-day life-style—preferring to be decisive and planned (Judging, abbreviated by "J") or flexible and spontaneous (Perceiving, abbreviated by "P").

    J—"Let's decide to be there at 1:00 a.m. sharp."
    P—"Let's get there in the early afternoon unless something else comes along."

These four concepts apply to all people alike. The four concepts or dimensions can be described in terms of preferences—two opposites for each dimension. We all have eight dimensions but we prefer and find it easier to use only four. It is like being right-handed and throwing a ball. You do better throwing it with your right hand; you could do it with your left, but it would be more difficult and you would not be as accurate.

DIRECTIONS

1. Read the list of questions which follows.

2. Check each item that applies to you.

    a. Do I . . .
        ____ demonstrate energy and enthusiasm?
        ____ respond quickly without needing to think?
        ____ act quickly before thinking?
        ____ talk and think at the same time?
        ____ get tired if activities are long and slow?
        ____ talk a lot?
        ____ seem to have many friends?
        ____ learn best by interaction?
        ____ learn best by hearing?
        ____ share emotions and thoughts as they occur?
        ____ seem able to do many things at the same time?
        ____ scatter energy?
        ____ seem to jump from one thought to another without going deeply into the subject?

        These are some of the traits shown by **"Extroverts."** Thus when someone exhibits these traits, they are extroverted and often their energy comes from the outer world of people.

    b. Do I . . .
        ____ need to know you before I trust you?
        ____ prefer to work or play one-on-one as opposed to in groups?

____ think for a long time and then maybe act?
____ work or play alone patiently for a long time?
____ enjoy learning by reading or visual cues?
____ keep things to himself or herself?
____ hesitate somewhat before tying something new?
____ seem to have a few close friends?
____ prefer to work in a quiet place?
____ appear to bottle up emotions?
____ think about a topic very deeply before going on to the next topic?
____ typically not volunteer information in a meeting or class?
____ concentrate energy?

These are some of the traits of an **"Introvert."** If you see someone exhibiting these traits, they are probably introverted and obtain their energy from their inner world of thought and ideas.

c. Do I. . .
____ like to be shown facts, details, and examples?
____ enjoy familiar activities and routines?
____ approach things in a step by step fashion?
____ observe and remember details?
____ memorize easily?
____ enjoy working with my hands?
____ seem steady and patient?
____ prefer things being presented in a short, succinct style?
____ operates from real life experience and practicality?
____ likes things in writing?

These are traits of **"Sensing"** types. Thus when someone is exhibiting these traits, they are perceiving through their senses. They are step-by-step, practical, realistic people.

d. Do I. . .
____ want to hear the main idea first?
____ work in spurts, not an even flow?
____ enjoy learning new things?
____ enjoy being different?
____ look at the big picture first?
____ have a vivid imagination?
____ often lose things?
____ quickly go from one thing to another?
____ work and play in fits and starts?

These are traits of **"Intuitive"** types. Thus when someone exhibits these traits they are perceiving through their intuition. These people are often futuristic and visionary.

e. Do I. . .

_____ ask "Why" a lot?

_____ insist on logical explanations?

_____ like to arrange things in orderly patterns?

_____ show more interest in ideas than people?

_____ stress the importance of fairness?

_____ like recognition for doing things well?

_____ believe strongly in things?

_____ spend time thinking about things?

_____ offer brief and concise statements?

_____ come across as critical?

_____ appear calm in crisis?

These are traits of **"Thinking"** types. Thus when some exhibits these traits, they are making decision based on an objective thought process.

f. Do I. . .

_____ like to know the other person before doing business?

_____ like to talk or read about people?

_____ want to be praised for caring for others?

_____ wants to help if someone is unhappy?

_____ tell stories expressively, in great detail?

_____ try to be tactful?

_____ want to be told I am loved and cared for?

_____ relate well with people?

These are some of the traits of **"Feeling"** types. Thus if someone exhibits these traits, they might be making decision based on personal feelings.

g. Do I . . .

_____ like timetables?

_____ not like last-minute changes?

_____ like to know what is going to happen in the future?

_____ enjoy choices and closure?

_____ give timeliness to myself?

_____ like to set goals?

_____ have definite opinions?

_____ do best with deadlines?

_____ like to be in charge?

_____ like to make decisions and continue on with the task?

_____ like to meet someone at 8:00 a.m. sharp?

These are some of the traits of a **"Judging"** type. Thus when you observe someone exhibiting these traits, they are relating to the world through their judging function and typically prefer life to be orderly and well-planned.

h. Do I . . .

____ like spontaneity?

____ show curiosity?

____ become energized by new ideas and experiences?

____ have a difficult time with deadlines?

____ often perceive work as play?

____ appear open to new ideas?

____ rush to meet deadlines?

____ like to get more information before making a decision?

____ like options?

____ enjoy autonomy?

____ always seem to need more information before making a decision?

____ like to see you sometime tomorrow?

These are some of the traits of a **"Perceiving"** type. Thus when someone exhibits these traits, he or she is relating to the world through their perceiving function and typically prefers a life-style that is flexible and spontaneous.

3. Count the number of items you checked and record numbers in the appropriate space provided.

E Total ____   I Total ____

S Total ____   N Total ____

T Total ____   F Total ____

J Total ____   P Total ____

A Summary of my preference so far is (circle one letter in each of four pairs)

E or I   S or N   T or F   J or P

Note: This checklist is not meant to replace a professionally administered and interpreted Myers-Briggs Type Indicator.

4. Check the words in the following categories that are most appropriate for you.

Here are some key words to describe how Extroverts and Introverts differ.

Extroverts (E)

___ Social
___ Talkative
___ Externally focused
___ Many things at once
___ Many friends
___ Expend energy
___ Outgoing
___ Speak and maybe Think
___ Action

Total E words checked _____.

Introverts (I)

___ Solitary
___ Quiet
___ Internally focused
___ Depth
___ Deep into one thing
___ Deep friendships
___ Preserve energy
___ Thinking
___ Think and then may speak
___ Reaction

Total I words checked _____.

Enter which one had the most checked.
Ex: E - 4, I - 2, Preference is E.

Preference _____.

Here are some key words to describe Sensors and Intuitive types.

Sensors (S)

___ To the point
___ Here and now
___ Concrete
___ Toil
___ Actual
___ Feet on the ground
___ Facts
___ Practical
___ Step-by-step

____ Specific
____ Experience

Total S words checked _____.

Intuitive types (N)
____ Around the point
____ Future
____ Concept
____ Inspiration
____ Possible
____ Head in the clouds
____ Dreams
____ Fantasy
____ Jump to conclusions
____ Overview
____ Hunches

Total N words checked _____.

Preference _____.

Here are some key words to describe how Feelers and Thinkers differ.

Thinkers (T)
____ Head
____ Laws
____ Fairness
____ Objective
____ Clear
____ Detached
____ Just
____ Logical
____ Principals
____ Impersonal
____ Critique

Total T words checked _____.

Feelers (F)
____ Heart
____ Situation

___ Persuade

___ Subjective

___ Fuzzy

___ Involved

___ Humane

___ Sentimental

___ Values

___ Personal

___ Appreciate

Total F words checked _____.

Preference _____.

Here are some key words to describe how Judgers and Perceivers differ.

Judgers (J)

___ Analyze

___ Order

___ Settled

___ Decided

___ Fixed

___ Closure

___ Timetable

___ Scheduled

___ Deadline

___ Decisive

___ Control

___ Plan Ahead

___ Structured

Total J words checked _____.

Perceivers (P)

___ Options

___ Appears disorganized

___ Pending

___ Wait and see

___ Flexible

___ Open-ended

___ Tentative

___ Spontaneous

___ What deadline?

___ Changeable

___ Adapt

Name _____

Date _____ Hour _____

____ Adapt as you go
____ Unstructured

Total P words checked _____.

Preference _____.

5. Transfer your preferences to the following (circle one letter in each pair):

E or I
S or N
T or F
J or P

Look at the eight preferences as listed, two for each dimension. These eight preferences are expressed in individual words and abbreviated by a letter for each.

Dimension	Preferences and Abbreviations	
ENERGY SOURCE	[I] INTROVERSION (Personal reflections) Inside of self	[E] EXTROVERSION (From people and ideas) Outside of self
GATHERING INFORMATION	[N] INTUITION (From the sixth or intuitive sense) Figurative, random	[S] SENSING (From the five senses) Literal orsequential
MAKE DECISIONS	[F] FEELING (Personal and affect-oriented) Subjective and interpersonally	[T] THINKING (Abstract and objective) Impersonal
DAY-TO-DAY LIVING	[P] PERCEIVING Flexible and spontaneous	[J] JUDGING Orderly, planned, and decisive

6. Review the following summary of the eight types now that you have tallied your tentative profile.

7. If a difference exists between your first profile from Direction 3 and Direction 4, review preferences to see if you are somewhat tentative on your choices. If so, this may only reflect a transition or a flexible state as far as that type is concerned at this time.

8. List your best fit Type expressed in four letters based on
    a. Your results after having completed the previous seven directions.
    b. Your assessment type if you took the MBTI.

Item 3	☐	☐	☐	☐
Item 4	☐	☐	☐	☐
MBTI	☐	☐	☐	☐

My Best Fit

☐	☐	☐	☐

9. Identify a person that you know who has a type different from yours and review how this difference or these differences affect you.

_____

_____

HOMEWORK

Study Exercise 2.5 and complete the first six directions before the next group meeting.

> "A moment's insight is sometimes worth a life's experience."
> Oliver Wendell Holmes, 1860

Exercise 2.5

Name _____

Date _____ Hour _____

MY STRENGTHS AND BLIND SPOTS

Based on information concerning your own type, the next step is to recognize the strengths and blind spots of each of your preferences.

GOAL

In this exercise you will come to know better your strengths and blind spots.

DIRECTIONS

1. Review the list of possible strengths and blind spots of each preference.

Type	Strengths	Blind Spots
E	Meet people easily Have a gift of gab Can do multiple things at once Think out loud Talk my way through conflict	Don't listen Appear shallow
I	Think before speaking Examine things in depth	Appear shy Avoid conflict Prefer one person May not consider the obvious
S	Approach things in a step-by-step fashion Focus on here and now Am excellent with details	May not see the big picture See just the present
N	See the big picture Focus on the future Look at possibilities	Lose sight of the facts Have too many ideas Am stressed because of all ideas
T	Am logical Am rational Use logistics Am task-oriented Bring objectivity to a problem	Are not considerate of others Fear losing control Appear detached and cold

F		
	Consider people issues	Seem fuzzy-headed
	Am sensitive	Can personalize conflict
	Like harmony	Hurt easily
	Consider how a decision will affect others	

J		
	Am quick to make decisions	May not have enough information before I decide
	Work steadily on a project	Can be rigid
	Am good at structure	Become frustrated with change

P		
	Go with the flow	Am late with projects
	Gather lots of information before making a decision	Do last minute rush
	Handle change well	Am distracted by others' options
	Am always open for other's options	

2. Underline those strengths and blind spots that apply to you.

3. Ask others who know you well to read your self-assessment and give you feedback.

4. Write a paragraph describing your strengths and blind spots.

_____

_____

_____

_____

5. Identify those strengths that you would bring to a peer helping group.

_____

_____

6. List why you need people with different preferences in your group.

_____

_____

7. Share what you have learned about yourself.

HOMEWORK

Study Exercise 2.6 before the next group meeting.

Name _____

Date _____ Hour _____

LEARNING HOW TO APPRECIATE OTHERS WHO ARE DIFFERENT

Conflict appears to be a way of life today. Groups can be both frustrating and stress-producing. As you begin to understand type, you may begin to see difficulties as a result of type differences as opposed to "real differences." If we learn to appreciate others, we need to understand the ways people like to be appreciated. Some may like compliments, others may like to just have fun.

GOAL

In this exercise you will learn how to appreciate others who are different from you.

DIRECTIONS

1. Divide into two groups: one group of Extroverts and one group of Introverts.

   a. Brainstorm within each group how you like to be appreciated.

      Examples: Extroverts like to talk about things.
                Introverts like to see things in writing.

   b. Report on a large piece of newsprint the brainstorming ideas so you
      can them share later.

   c. Have the two groups share what they came up with.

2. Divide into two groups: one group of Intuitives and one group of Sensors.

   a. Brainstorm how you like to be appreciated.

   b. Write on newsprint the brainstorming ideas to share later.

   c. Have the two groups share.

3. Divide into two groups: one group of Thinkers and one group of Feelers.

   a. Brainstorm how you like to be appreciated.

b. Write on newsprint the brainstorming ideas to share later.

c. Have the two groups share.

4. Divide into two groups: one group of Judgers and one group of Perceivers.

a. Brainstorm how you like to be appreciated.

b. Write on newsprint the brainstorming ideas to share later.

c. Have the two groups share.

5. Divide into pairs. Make sure the two people are different or somewhat different.

Examples: ENTJ and ISFP
INTJ and ENTP

6. Role-play a statement of appreciation to someone who is different using what you have just learned about different types.

7. Receive feedback from your partner, who is different, about how your appreciation was received.

HOMEWORK

1. Think about and then record how you could use your appreciation skills in helping others.

_____

_____

_____

_____

2. Study Exercise 2.7 and complete as much as possible before the next group meeting.

Name _____

Date _____ Hour _____

COMMUNICATING WITH THOSE DIFFERENT FROM YOU

As you start to work with those different from you, you will become aware that you need to learn not only basic helping skills (attending, empathy, summarizing, genuineness, assertiveness, questioning, confrontation, problem solving, conflict mediation) but also to recognize that at times others appear to be on a different "wavelength." The intent of this exercise is to help you as you work not only with your peer helping group but also with the people whom you will try to help.

GOAL

In this exercise you will learn to communicate better with people different from you.

DIRECTIONS

1. Find your type among the brief descriptions of the sixteen types.

2. Compare your type to the opposite type.

3. Consider how well you understand and communicate with your opposite type.

4. Recognize how developing the qualities of your opposite would be difficult. Would doing so be rewarding?

BRIEF DESCRIPTIONS OF THE SIXTEEN TYPES*

ENTJ
Intuitive, innovative ORGANIZER; analytic, systematic, confident; pushed to get action on new ideas and challenges.

ESTJ
Fact-minded practical ORGANIZER; assertive analytic, systematic; pushes to get things done and working smoothly and efficiently.

INTP
Inquisitive ANALYZER; reflective, independent, curious, more interested in organizing ideas than situations or people.

ISTP
Practical ANALYZER; values exactness; more interested in organizing data than situations or people; reflective, a cool and curious observer of life.

ESTP
REALISTIC ADAPTER in the world of material things; good-natured, tolerant, easy-going, oriented to practical, firsthand experience; highly observant of details of things.

ESFP
REALISTIC ADAPTER in human relationships; friendly and easy with people, highly observant of their feelings and needs; oriented to practical, firsthand experience.

ISTJ
Analytical MANAGER OF FACTS AND DETAILS; dependable, decisive, painstaking and systematic; concerned with systems and organization; stable and conservative.

ISFJ
Sympathetic MANAGER OF FACTS AND DETAILS,concerned with people's welfare; dependable, painstaking and systematic: stable and conservative.

ISFP
Observant, loyal HELPER; reflective, realis-, tic empathic; patient with details, gentle and retiring; shuns disagreements; enjoys the moment.

INFP
Imaginative, independent HELPER; reflective, inquisitive, empathic, loyal to ideals; more interested in possibilities than practicalities.

ESFJ
Practical HARMONIZER and worker-with-people; sociable, orderly, opinioned; conscientious, realistic and well tuned to the here and now.

ENFJ
Imaginative HARMONIZER and worker-with-people; sociable, expressive, orderly, opinioned. conscientious; curious about new ideas and possibilities.

INFJ
People-oriented INNOVATOR of ideas; serious, quietly forceful and persevering; concerned with the common good, with helping others develop.

INTJ
Logical, critical, decisive INNOVATOR of serious ideas; serious, intent, highly independent,concerned with organization; determined and often stubborn.

ENFP
Warmly enthusiastic PLANNER OF CHANGE; imaginative, individualistic; pursues inspirationwith impulsive energy; seeks to understand and inspire others.

ENTP
Inventive, analytical PLANNER OF CHANGE; enthusiastic and independent; pursues inspiration with impulsive energy; seeks to understand and inspire others.

---

*From Gordon D. Lawrence, *People and Tiger Stripes*, (3rd ed.), 1993. Published by Center for Applications of Psychological Type, 1-800-777-2278. Used by permission of the author.

5. Read the comments below as to how people of different preferences like to be communicated with.

HOW TO COMMUNICATE WITH OTHERS

E

Be spontaneous.
Show enthusiasm.
Be open with your communication.
Focus on the external world.

I

Write it out first.
Give them time to know you first.
Make a agenda.
Allow them time to think before speaking.
Allow time to process.

S

Show facts first.
Be practical.
Be direct.
Show step by step.

N

Present the big picture first.
Are not interested in details.
Indicate the possibilities.
Work in bursts rather than steady pace.
Show what is nonroutine.

T

Be logical.

Get the point.
Be calm and reasonable.
Show that feelings are really facts.

F

Spend time getting to know them first.
Allow time to discuss thoroughly.
Show why valuable to people.
Watch body language.
Show how you agree.
Use empathy.

J

Present a time table and stick to it.
Give Judgers warnings.
Allow time to prepare.
Show results.
Take a stand.

P

Allow things to flow.
Bring in new information.
Allow for options and changes.
Encourage autonomy.
Allow for last-minute rush.
Allow for changes in directions.

---

6. Practice with a partner different from you the following situations:

a. You are to convince one of your fellow trainees about joining you in a volunteer activity.

b. You are going to try to sell your trainer on the idea of a party for the trainees.

7. Give feedback to the person doing the talking.

HOMEWORK

1. Observe another person (friend, family member) and then try to communicate differently using type information.

2. Prepare for next session, Exercise 2.8.

> *"For most people, really understanding their own type in particular, and other people's types in general, is a releasing experience rather than a restricting one. It sets one free to recognize one's own natural bent and to trust one's own potential for growth and excellence, with no obligation to copy anyone else, however admirable that person may be in his or her own different way."*
>
> *Isabell Myers*

Exercise 2.8

KNOWING MY HERITAGE

GOAL

In this exercise you will come to know better some things that influence who you are today.

DIRECTIONS

1. On the back side of this sheet, draw a picture, or pictures of things that represent information about the culture you are from.

2. Share these pictures with your group.

3. Discuss how people of different cultures are alike, and how they are different.

    a. How are people more alike than different?

    b. How can different ways of being and behavior be an asset to society?

4. Identify other cultures in the populations with whom you may be working.

    _____

    _____

    _____

    _____

5. Discuss implications of those differences for peer helpers.

HOMEWORK:

1. Try to learn about others' cultures by talking to friends and coworkers.

2. Read introduction to Module III and Exercise 3.1 before the next group meeting.

MODULE III

Let's Look at Helping

LET'S LOOK AT HELPING

Helping involves others. This module is designed to increase your awareness of several characteristics of the helping process. In this module you, the trainee, will explore certain behaviors that make a much better helper.

Friendships can result in either healthy or unhealthy influences. You will have an opportunity to examine how friendships have influenced you in a healthy or unhealthy manner.

To establish a measurement of your ability to be a helper, you will identify behaviors of helping that you like or dislike in other people. Then you will identify similar behaviors of your own and become aware of effective and ineffective helping behaviors.

You will identify persons who have come to you with a problem and identify the behaviors you exhibited as you listened and helped these individuals. You will discuss with the other trainees your interactions with persons who came to you. Through the discussion you will be able to establish how you succeed as a helper. You will have a chance to remember your favorite helper.

Use: Exercise 3.1 is best used with youth.
Exercise 3.2 may be helpful for adults.
Exercises 3.3, 3.4, 3.5, and 3.6 are useful for both youth and adults.

Name _____

Date _____ Hour _____

THE POWER OF PEERS

In our society, we are often influenced the most by our peers--our friends and people we are around most.

GOAL

In this exercise you will identify how peers influence you in healthy and unhealthy manners.

DIRECTIONS

1. Think about a current or former peer (example: friend or coworker) who influenced you to get involved in a unhealthy manner (example: getting you involved with alcohol).

    a. What did you learn from that friend?

    b. How did that behavior make you feel?

    c. How did others react to you?

2. Think about a current or former peer (friend or coworker) that influenced you to get involved in a healthy manner (example: exercising).

    a. What did you learn from that friend?

    b. How did that behavior make you feel?

    c. How did others react to you?

3. Discuss the power of peers.

HOMEWORK

1. Think about peers that you now have and how they have influenced you.

2. Write your ideas in the boxes.

Had a Healthy Influence	Had an Unhealthy Influence

Exercise 3.2

Name _____

Date _____ Hour _____

IMAGING MY HELPER

In our life, each of us has known someone, such as a parent, relative, friend, co-worker, or boss who has helped us or others. In this exercise you will spend just a few minutes thinking about those persons and what behaviors they did that were helpful.

GOAL

In this exercise you will come to understand better behaviors of helpers.

DIRECTIONS

1. Listen to your trainer lead you through an imagery exercise to imagine your helper.

2. Draw a picture or write phrases that represent your helper.

My Image of a Helper

3. Answer the following questions.

   a. How strong was the image? _____

   _____

   b. What behavior did you observe? _____

   _____

   c. How did he or she make you feel? _____

   _____

   d. What did you learn?_____

   _____

4. List characteristics that you saw in your helper, and then discuss with your training

   group._____

   _____

HOMEWORK

1. Develop a definition of helping.

2. Read and complete as much of Exercise 3.3 as possible before the next group meeting.

Exercise 3.3

Name _____

Date _____ Hour _____

EXPLORING HELPING BEHAVIORS IN OTHERS

Certain behaviors make you a much better helper. In observing others who help you, you will notice the importance of such characteristics as how well others listen to you, give attention to you, are honest, and so forth. In order for you to become aware of how you relate to others in a helping role, let's explore those behaviors of others in relation to you.

GOALS

In this exercise you will learn

1. to become aware of helping behaviors that you like in others and those you dislike, and

2. to become aware of effective and ineffective behaviors.

DIRECTIONS

1. Before the next meeting of your training group, please list on the next page three people with whom you enjoyed talking and sharing problems in the past.

2. Under the name of each person listed, place a check mark beside the skills and personal behavior characteristics you liked in that person.

3. Be prepared to discuss in the group training session reasons for the placement of your check marks.

4. Try to brainstorm all behaviors that seem to be helpful to you.

People with whom I
shared my problems
_____   _____   _____

Paid attention to me
(looked at me)
_____   _____   _____

Seemed to hear me
_____   _____   _____

I can trust the person
to keep a secret
_____   _____   _____

Didn't joke about my
problem
_____   _____   _____

Was honest with me
about my problem
_____   _____   _____

The person was open
in describing own
feelings
_____   _____   _____

Understood what I
said
_____   _____   _____

Other characteristics
I liked (please list)

_____   _____   _____   _____

_____   _____   _____   _____

5. In the space provided below describe behaviors, both verbal and nonverbal,
that are important for you to do as a good listener.

_____

_____

_____

_____

HOMEWORK

1. Practice the helping behaviors you identified.
2. Complete Exercise 3.4.

Exercise 3.4

Name _____

Date _____ Hour _____

HOW DO I HELP?

You as a helper to others will be effective as you display behavior characteristics liked by others. Let's look at you as you relate to others in a helping role by completing the following exercise.

GOALS

In this exercise you will learn

1. to become aware of your helping characteristics that others like.

2. to recognize characteristics of behaviors that are effective and ineffective in helping others.

DIRECTIONS

1. Before the next meeting of your training group, identify on the next page people who come to you with a problem.

2. Place a check mark beside those behaviors you used with each person identified.

3. Be prepared to discuss your placement of the check marks.

4. Analyze your check marks for Exercises 3.3 and 3.4 to determine what you consider to be effective helping behaviors.

Names of persons coming
to you with a problem   _____   _____

_____

<u>My</u> <u>Behaviors</u>

I looked at them   _____   _____

I attempted to understand
problem completely   _____   _____

I let them know I understood   _____   _____

I reported my feelings honestly   _____   _____

I helped them find solutions   _____   _____

I considered the problem
seriously   _____   _____

Other behaviors (please list):

_____   _____   _____

When people came to me with a problem, I interacted with them by (please describe):

_____

_____

HOMEWORK

Review Exercise 3.5 and complete through Direction 2 before the next group meeting.

Exercise 3.5

Name _____

Date _____ Hour _____

HELPING THROUGH SERVICE TO OTHERS

Most of us have been in a helping role in the past by giving our time for others or for a cause. Service is the backbone of our society.

GOAL

In this exercise you will identify volunteer work you have done in the past and would like to do in the future.

DIRECTIONS

1. List examples of ways that you have volunteered your time to help others for some kind of cause (example: helped a child learn math, helped collect funds for American Cancer Society).

2. Answer the following questions:
   a. How did that make you feel?

   _____

   _____

   b. What did you learn from that experience?

   _____

   _____

   c. What kind of service work would you like to perform in the future?

   _____

   _____

3. Discuss your SERVICE WORK with your training group.

HOMEWORK

Review Exercise 3.6 and come prepared to do the exercise during the group meeting.

Exercise 3.6

Name _____

Date _____ Hour _____

PRACTICE IN HELPING

An important way to learn helpful behaviors is to start using them in the training group with others who also are learning and wanting to practice. This activity will be fun as you begin looking at helping behaviors.

GOALS

In this exercise you will learn

1. to practice helping behaviors.

2. to give feedback concerning helping behavior.

DIRECTIONS A

1. Divide into clusters of three.

2. Have the helpee discuss an issue for two to three minutes; have another person provide the listener feedback.

3. As feedback provider, use the check sheet on the next page to mark the listener's behaviors. Use your notes after the discussion to provide feedback for listeners.

4. Change roles and repeat directions in Number 2.

5. Change roles again so that each of you have been a helpee (discussant), a listener, and a feedback provider.

6. Discuss the experience in the total group.

LISTENER'S BEHAVIORS

DIRECTIONS B

1. When you serve in the feedback provider role, please check those behaviors you observed in the listener.

Feedback for Listener

_____ Looked at person with problem.

_____ Attempted to understand problem.

_____ Let the other person know he/she was understood.

_____ Reported honest feelings.

_____ Helped to find a solution.

_____ Treated problem seriously.

Other(s) _____

_____

_____

_____

---

2. After the helpee (discussant) and listener have finished, provide feedback to the listener as to behaviors you observed.

HOMEWORK

1. Review Module IV and bring Exercise 4.1 completed to the next group meeting.

2. Come prepared to do Exercise 4.2 during the next group meeting.

MODULE IV

Communication Stoppers

MODULE **IV**

COMMUNICATION STOPPERS

In day-to-day living we have a desire to express our problems, needs, and wants. We need and want to be heard and understood by others. Because of our need to talk out our problems, we seek out people we think can help. Those people we ask to help usually are willing to try but often they do not have those skills needed to assist effectively. Few people have learned good helping skills, and as a result, they respond in ways that meet their own needs but which often are different from needs of those they are trying to help. People who are trying to help respond to our pleas for help with behaviors that they have learned randomly by just being around other people, but frequently leave the person they are trying to help frustrated and unsatisfied. Several "helpful" behaviors that many people use when asked to be a helper are simply common and expected expressions.

Recently, research has been designed to study just how effective these "helpful" behaviors really are in their ability to assist people. Surprisingly, these studies have found that those behaviors are not helpful, and in fact, often are quite harmful both to the helper and the helpee.

Our firm belief is that everyone can learn to communicate better. Specific techniques, if used, will most certainly improve your ability to "give and receive information." A first step is to be aware of some communication stoppers that we may all use at one time or another. We shall identify some common communication stoppers in exercises within this module.

In Module IV the exercises show how some often-used socalled "helping" behaviors really are not helping. Thus, you can recognize and eliminate the undesirable ones. This recognition is needed before other effective behaviors can be learned. These ineffective "helping" behaviors are what we call communication stoppers.

Communication stoppers are helper behaviors, which although they appear to be helpful, are really responses that are negative in effect and retard helpful interpersonal relationships.

Communication stoppers, regardless of words used, all send an undesirable message to the helpee. In this module are shown those messages and why they are not helping behaviors. All communication stoppers have the following qualities in common:

- Each communication stopper is a "put down" to the helpee in some way.

- Each communication stopper is ineffective in its ability to solve problems or help the helpee to feel better.

- Each communication stopper makes the relationship worse by causing the helpee to close off from the helper or to cause the helpee to withdraw from further exploration of the concern.

- Each communication stopper causes separation of people rather than closeness.

As helpers, avoid words that stop communication. The following two exercises will alert you to some frequently used phrases that interfere with a helping process. Those stoppers listed obviously are not a complete list but are the more common or destructive ones. An awareness of these and other stoppers will help you recognize what phrases to avoid in relating to others; however, at times you want to use the stoppers. (see Exercise 4.3)

The goal of peer helper training is to teach you phrases that encourage others to communicate to you in a meaningful way. By avoiding communication stoppers, your chances of being an effective listener are increased.

Use: This exercise is best used with high school and older students.

Name _____

Date _____ Hour _____

RECOGNIZING COMMUNICATION STOPPERS

GOAL

In this exercise you will learn to identify communications that are not helpful.

DIRECTIONS

1. Study the definition for each of the eleven communication stoppers.

2. Read the sample statement that illustrates the communication stopper.

3. Think of other responses that are examples of communication stoppers.

4. Write in the space provided examples of each behavior that if given in a conversation would produce communication stoppage.

EXERCISE, TERMS, AND DEFINITIONS

1. **Directing, ordering**: To tell someone to do something in such a manner that gives the other person little or no choice.

   Sample Statements: "Shut the door."
                        "Do the dishes."

   Examples:
   1a. _____

   _____

   1b. _____

   _____

2. **Warning, threatening**: To tell the other person that if the behavior continues, certain consequences will happen.

   Sample Statements: "Stop making fun of me or I'll leave."
                        "If you continue drinking, you'll be an alcoholic."

Examples:
   2a. _____

   _____

   2b. _____

   _____

3. **Moralizing, preaching:** To tell someone things they ought to do.

Sample Statements: "You should be kind to older people."
"You should make good grades to get ahead."

Examples:
3a. _____

_____

3b. _____

_____

4. **Persuading, arguing:** To try to influence another person with facts, information, and logic.

Sample Statements: "This paper is better because it has wider lines on it."
"You should quit smoking because it causes heart problems and respiratory problems."

Examples:
4a. _____

_____

4b. _____

_____

5. **Advising, recommending:** To provide answers for a problem.

Sample Statements: "I recommend that you take algebra."
"I would advise you to take that job because it pays well."

Examples:
5a. _____

_____

5b. _____

_____

6. **Evaluating, criticizing:** To make a negative interpretation of someone's behavior.

Sample Statements: "You walk too slowly."
"You didn't do a good job of straightening the garage."

Examples:
6a. _____

6b. _____

_____

7. **Praising:** To make a positive evaluation of someone's behavior.

Sample Statements: "You smile at the right times."
"You always know the right thing to say in a situation."

Examples:
7a. _____

_____

7b. _____

_____

8. **Supporting, sympathizing:** To try to talk individuals out of their feelings or to deny their feelings.

Sample Statements: "I've been there; I know how you feel."
"Your problem is really serious; I can imagine how you feel."

Examples:
8a. _____

_____

8b. _____

_____

9. **Diagnosing:** To analyze persons' behavior and communicate that you have figured out their behavior.

Sample Statements: "You must be high on something because your eyes are red."
"You must be depressed because you're not eating."

Examples:
9a. _____

_____

9b. _____

_____

10. **Diverting, bypassing:** To change the subject or talk about issues presented by other individuals.

Sample Statements: "I know you're upset about your family, but let me tell you about my car problems."
"I don't think that grade is that bad; you wouldn't believe the grade I got in that class—an A+!"

Examples:
10a. _____

_____

10b. _____

_____

11. **Kidding, teasing:** To try to avoid talking about the problem by laughing or by distracting the individual you are addressing.

Sample Statements: "You're really a top-flight egghead to be taken in by that guy."
"Let me cheer you and tell you a joke I just heard."

Examples:
11a. _____

_____

11b. _____

_____

HOMEWORK

1. Study Exercise 4.2 and complete it before the next group meeting.

2. Study Exercise 4.3, complete it, and come to the next group meeting prepared to do it.

Name _____

Date _____ Hour _____

IDENTIFYING COMMUNICATION STOPPERS IN CERTAIN RESPONSES

GOAL

In this exercise you will learn to identify communication stoppers in specific responses.

DIRECTIONS

1. Refer to the list of communications stoppers in Exercise 4.1 and review the eleven different kinds of stoppers.

2. Decide what kind of stopper is being used in each example shown on the next page.

3. Write the number of the communication stopper from Exercise 4.1 on the line preceeding each example in the following exercise to show the corresponding kind (terminology) of communication stopper which has been used.

DIFFERENT KINDS OF STOPPERS

___1. "People who cry are just 'wimps;' come on you don't want to be a wimp— the tears are going to cause a flood."

___2. "I know you have a problem with your girlfriend, but let me tell you about my girlfriend, she is super and considerate."

___3. "When you come in with those watery eyes, I think you must have been smoking pot."

___4. "I feel so sorry for you that you can't learn math, you are really in bad shape, poor you. . ."

___5. "You are the greatest artist in the whole world. You picture is beautiful. You should be famous.

___6. "You dummy, why can't you figure out your English. Speaking is so simple, and you are really stupid not to understand it."

___7. "I definitely would advise you to not take that job because you don't like math and have never done well in a job that involves math."

___8. "You should paint your room because of the following reasons:
a. So it will look better,
b. It will look new,
c. I like it, and so forth."

__9. "You should stop smoking because it is so bad for your health. You will probably have cancer by the time you are thirty."

__10. "If you come in late tomorrow, your pay will be docked."

__11. "Do your work!!"

HOMEWORK

See homework at close of Exercise 4.1.

Exercise 4.3

Name _____

Date _____ Hour _____

STOPPERS O.K. AT TIMES!

At times, you may decide that you do not want to be in a role as a helper or a good listener. You may simply want information or to give confirmation

GOAL

In this exercise you will identify appropriate times to use stoppers.

DIRECTIONS

1. Consider times when you may want to use communication stoppers. Please write them in the space provided.

   Example: Don't run in the street.

   _____

   _____

   _____

   _____

2. Identify some roles you are in when you are not a helper or a listener.

   Example: Working on a computer

   _____

   _____

   _____

   _____

HOMEWORK

1. Read the introduction to Module V.

2. Review Exercise 5.1 and complete it before the next group meeting.

Unit **B**

DEVELOPING

SKILLS

DEVELOPING SKILLS

Problems in communication often result from poor listening and responding skills. Although attentive listening seems like a simple thing to do, we take it for granted. Attentive listening requires both the desire and the skill. Unit A, **Setting the Stage,** helped you identify your desire and Unit B, **Developing Skills,** will assist you in learning listening and responding skills. When others feel understood, it is both satisfying and helpful to them. This is true regardless of culture, age, and gender. When people feel they have been heard, a reduction occurs in the distance between the talker and the listener.

Unit B, **Developing Skills,** will help you learn **Attending** skills (Module V) which will focus on the nonverbal behaviors that let a person know you are listening. One of the most difficult listening skills to learn is **Empathy** (Module VI) because it involves accurately hearing the content and feelings of another person. Some of you will find listening for content easier than listening for feelings. Others will find hearing feelings easier than content. The exercises within the module will help you learn effective Empathy skills in a step-by-step manner. At times, it is helpful for you to **Summarize** (Module VII) and put in your own words what the helpee has said. Therefore, your ability to see the "big picture" and give feedback to the helpee helps him/her understand self better.

Module VIII will help you ask **questions** when it is important that you try to help understand the person and learn more about them. At times another person's behavior may be causing you problems, therefore you need to learn how to be **Genuine** (Module IX) in listening and responding. Being genuine is a model for the helpee to follow and facilitate growth. You may need to express some of what you want in such a manner that gets your point across but respects others. **Assertiveness Skills** which are presented in Module X can be helpful at home and at work.

At times, situations may occur in which others' behavior is causing you a problem and it is destructive for them. The skill of **Confrontation** (Module XI) will be helpful for you to learn how to intervene with others when they are involved in unhealthy behaviors.

Sometimes, helpees may need help at **Problem Solving,** (Module XII). Work groups and/or family groups, that can solve problems, function more efficiently, experience less stress, and are more productive. Individuals that solve a major problem often feel relieved.

These basic listening and responding skills will give you a foundation to perform a variety of peer helping activities.

> *"Half the misery in the world comes of want of courage to speak and to hear the truth plainly, and in a spirit of love."*
>
> Harriet Beecher Stowe

MODULE V

Attending

The First Skill in Peer Helping

8
7
6
5
4
3
2
1 Attending

ATTENDING,
THE FIRST SKILL
IN PEER HELPING

One of the basic skills of listening and responding taught in the Peer Helper Training program is attending behavior. Attending skill communicates through using positive nonverbal signals the message that the helper is giving his/her undivided attention to the helpee.

Often our nonverbal signals give us away. Individuals communicate by tone of voice, eye contact, posture, and body movements. How we posture ourselves is a critical part of attending physically. Our physical posture communicates our readiness to respond to the other person's needs. These nonverbal signals give the impression that we are really listening in an attending way, only pretending that we are listening when we are not listening at all.

One easily recognizes when persons are not listening because they are obviously engaged in another activity. Sometimes individuals may be responding to us, but their nonverbal behavior says that they are a million miles away.

Nonverbal behaviors have more impact than what we say. What our bodies communicate is often more important than what we say. Based on statistical data, between 40 and 80% of our body language influences what people think! Our body language here includes our dress, posture, silence, facial expression, eye contact, and tone of voice.

Mehrabian (1969) argued that the total impact of a communication, or message, involved very little influence attributed to words spoken. Approximately 93% of a message impact is nonverbal!

ATTENDING SAYS "YOU ARE IMPORTANT"

The need for attention is a very real one: as tangible as is the need for food, for water, for shelter. Receiving attention from others is a form of reassurance. When we pay attention to another person we are in effect saying to the person, "You are real, you are important, you are here."

As a helping skill, attending involves various related processes. Perhaps above all, those wishing to help others must be able to attend physically. They must communicate in physical terms a desire to help individuals with whom they are working. Attending physically may involve the helper in one or more specific activities.

POSTURING

We communicate a great deal about our moods and attitudes through our postures. A couple listening to a symphony orchestra may lean back in their seats with their eyes closed; their posture indicates relaxation and absorption at the same time. But the interviewer who assumes the same posture when talking to an applicant about a job is signaling boredom and a lack of concern. This physical inclination of the body can signal a willingness to help—or a mental inclination that signals something entirely different.

MOVING

Another way that you can communicate helpful interest is through movement. The effect of a particular movement may be determined by the context in which it occurs. A drill sergeant advancing on a platoon of recruits may seem to his/her recruits to be threatening. In most other contexts, however, certainly in most helping situations, movement toward the individual will signal your increased interest and attention. By the same token, the movement may be away from the person whom you are helping and thus may signal disinterest.

HOLDING

Holding, touching, and simple physical contact can sometimes communicate a depth and intensity of concern when other modes of communication do not work. Holding is the most fundamental mode of attending; however, it is not, of course, appropriate to all helping situations. For one thing, physical contact of this sort is frequently associated with sexuality. And even if the person was "normal," had things "together," there always would be the chance that the person would be confused rather than comforted by such physical contact.

NOURISHING

Imagine a person sitting in a restaurant looking sad and depressed. Another person comes up to the individual and says, "Take this cup of coffee with sugar, you'll feel better." The common denominator is nourishment—one person's attending another by providing food or drink or shelter. In helping situations, providing nourishment may be done in physical and/or symbolic fashion.

Posturing, moving, holding, and nourishing are all ways in which we may communicate that we are attending physically. Physical attentiveness by itself, however, is not enough. We all probably have had the experience of talking to individuals who seemed to be attending, only to find out later that they had actually missed most of what we said. And in fairness, are not most of us adept at giving the appearance of attentiveness while our minds are actually far away? Attending physically is not enough. We must attend psychologically as well. In addition to exhibiting attentive patterns of physical behavior, we also must focus on the behavior and comments of those persons being helped. When we attend psychologically as well as physically we may best be described as communicating to the person as "hovering attentiveness." This can be accomplished in a number of different ways.

MAINTAINING EYE CONTACT

In the first place we must recognize the importance of eye contact. Our vision is perhaps our most important sense. We have all had the experience of talking to individuals who do not meet our gaze directly; we cannot tell whether they are listening to us or not. When we look directly into other persons' eyes, we let them know that we are giving them our full, undivided attention. This method of attending psychologically says to them: "I am here. I am aware of you. I care." To maintain eye contact does not mean staring at someone. Staring is too much eye contact!

OBSERVING AND LISTENING

Another method of attending psychologically involves observing. When we pay full attention to other persons, we take in a great deal of information about them because we are observing their behavior. For example, individuals who claim to be totally relaxed and yet chain-smoke one cigarette after another are exhibiting behavior at odds with their stated feelings. Listening completely involves paying attention and responding.

TENDING TO PEOPLE OF OTHER CULTURES

People have customs and mannerisms unique to their culture and ethnic group. As you begin to learn attending skills, please be sensitive to these different customs and mannerisms in such areas as eye contact, touch, and physical closeness.

For example, Sue and Sue (1990) indicated that white, middle class Americans avoid eye contact about 50% of the time when talking to others. However, when listening, they maintain eye contact more than 80% of the time. The opposite is true for most Black Americans who have greater eye contact when speaking and considerably less contact when listening. Another example is Navajo children who avoid eye contact with elders to show respect.

ATTENDING SKILL

Attending skill is extremely important in your day-to-day interaction with people. Often our thoughts and feelings affect our nonverbal behavior. When we posture ourselves for our own comfort and convenience we tend to think of ourselves; when we posture ourselves to attend to others we tend to think of them.

Often, if we are having certain thoughts, our nonverbal behavior is a giveaway. It is important and useful for all ages to learn this skill.

In helping young babies a helpful procedure is to hold and coddle them; they learn through physical contact that people care. As we grow older, physical contact is not as much a part of our interaction, but we still are quite aware of physical reaction. To learn the value of and the circumstances under which to use physical contact is useful for all ages.

An important behavior for a peer helper to learn is to send positive nonverbal signals. This first module on attending skill will make you aware of the importance of attending behavior and then will give you exercises to practice this skill.

Use. This module can be used for all age groups.

Exercise 5.1

Name _____

Date _____ Hour _____

EXAMPLES OF NONVERBAL COMMUNICATION BEHAVIORS

GOAL

In this exercise you will learn to recognize effective and ineffective nonverbal attending skills.

DIRECTIONS

1. Before the next meeting of your training group, complete the information requested on this exercise.

2. Under each of the headings, write your examples of nonverbal communication behaviors in the spaces provided.

3. For each example you write, identify whether you consider the behavior as effective (E), or ineffective (I). An example is provided for each heading. The "warm" examples are generally effective (E), and the "cold" examples are often ineffective (I).

NONVERBAL COMMUNICATION BEHAVIORS

1. Time

   Examples: Promptness in recognizing the presence of another (E). Delay in recognizing the presence of another (I).

   a. _____

   _____

   b. _____

   _____

2. Behaviors Using Body Language
   a. Eye Contact

      Examples: Warm—looking into another's eyes (E).
      Cold—avoiding looking at another (I).

      (1) _____

      (2) _____

      (3) _____

      (4) _____

b. Skin

Examples: Blushing (I)
Goose bumps (I)

(1) _____

(2) _____

(3) _____

(4) _____

c. Posture

Examples: Warm—eager, leaning toward (E)
Cold—leaning away (I), tense (I), hanging head (I), slouching (I)

(1) _____

(2) _____

(3) _____

(4) _____

d. Facial Expressions

Examples: Warm—smiling (E), interested (E)
Cold—frowning (I), disinterested (I)

(1) _____

(2) _____

(3) _____

(4) _____

e. Signs of Nervousness or Restlessness

Examples: Tapping fingers (I)
Biting nails (I)

(1) _____

(2) _____

(3) _____

(4) _____

f. Nonverbal Commands

   Examples: Holding finger to lips for silence (I)

   (1) _____

   (2) _____

   (3) _____

   (4) _____

3. Voice Inflections

   a. Tone of Voice

      Examples: Warm—soft (E)
                  Cold—hard (I)

      (1) _____

      (2) _____

   b. Rate of Speech

      Example: Fast (I)

      (1) _____

      (2) _____

   c. Loudness of Voice

      Examples: Soft (E)

      (1) _____

      (2) _____

   d. Diction

      Examples: Slurred (I)
                  Precise (E)

      (1) _____

      (2) _____

HOMEWORK

1. Come prepared at the next meeting to role-play a concern (a problem, real or imaginary). The role-playing is to be done in clusters of two, and the purpose is to provide experience for partners to practice attending skills.

2. Study and come prepared to discuss Exercise 5.2 at the next meeting.

Exercise 5.2

Name _____

Date _____ Hour _____

BECOMING AWARE OF MY ATTENDING BEHAVIOR

GOAL

In this exercise you will become better aware of effective and ineffective nonverbal behavior.

DIRECTIONS

1. Work with a partner who is presenting a problem and consciously avoid attending to the partner by not looking at the person, by doing other things—for example, by looking away while he/she is talking. Do this for a few minutes and then exchange roles.

2. Discuss with the total group how it felt to "not be attended to."

3. Work with the same partner; this time attend minimally to the partner and look at the person while your mind thinks of other things. Do this for a few minutes and then exchange roles.

4. Discuss with the total group your feelings concerning someone's minimally attending to you.

5. Now please attend completely to your partner. Through your posture, eye contact, and nonverbal behavior attend completely to the other person. Stick with this activity for a few minutes and then exchange partners.

6. Discuss how it felt to be attended to completely.

HOMEWORK

1. Observe people's attending behavior and the effects those behaviors have on other people.

2. Come to the next group meeting prepared to share and discuss your observations.

REACTIONS TO ATTENDING AWARENESS ACTIVITY

GOAL

In this exercise you will gain a better "feel" for what happens as a result of different attending activities by others to self (you).

DIRECTIONS

As a result of your experiences in the recent past, please write a response to the next seven directions:

1. Identify an experience in which someone else did not give you attending behaviors.

   _____

   _____

2. How did it feel to "not be attended to?"

   _____

   _____

3. Can you identify any reason as to why this "nonattending behavior may have occurred.

   _____

   _____

4. Identify an experience in which someone else showed some but only minimally attending behavior toward you.

   _____

   _____

5. How did it feel to be attended to minimally?

   _____

   _____

6. Identify an experience in which someone else gave you full attending behavior.

   _____

   _____

7. How did it feel to have someone attend completely to you?

_____

_____

8. Share with the group your comments on feelings received with the three levels of attending: nonattending, minimal attending, and attending behavior.

_____

_____

HOMEWORK

Observe the nonverbal behaviors of others and report these during the next group meeting.

BECOMING AWARE OF OTHERS' NONVERBAL BEHAVIOR

To become alert to the nonverbal behavior of others, you must use all your resources. You must use your senses, particularly your eyes. You must look for signals from other individuals. These signals will tell you if they are upset, happy, or are feeling other emotions. During this exercise, you will practice tuning in on the nonverbal behavior of others.

GOAL

During this exercise you will learn how to become alert to the nonverbal behavior of others.

DIRECTIONS

1. Select a partner and work as a team.

2. Assume roles as helper (one of the partners) and helpee (other partner). One of the two partners plays the role of the helpee; the other partner plays the role of the helper.

3. Play the role without talking. The persons playing the role of the helper should observe changes in the nonverbal behavior of the other. Look at the changes in color of skin, facial mannerisms, etc. Keep these changes in mind to share later.

4. As helpee, think the following thoughts:

   a. About something in your life that made you very happy. Try to imagine clearly the incident (1 minute).

   b. About something in your life that was very painful (1 minute).

   c. About something in your life of which you felt proud (1 minute).

5. As helper, describe to the helpee changes that were seen in nonverbal behavior. The helper might want to guess what the changes were.

HOMEWORK

1. After learning more about nonverbal behaviors, practice observing others to see how well you can pick up on those cues and their possible meanings.

2. Study Exercise 5.5 and complete Direction 1 before the next group meeting.

WORDS MEAN DIFFERENT THINGS TO DIFFERENT PEOPLE

As you are attending to others, knowing the meaning of terms utilized within their cultures is important so that you can acknowledge understanding.

GOAL

In this exercise you will focus on common language in your community.

DIRECTIONS

1. Look at the following list of words and write your definition:

   Ace Kool — _____

   _____

   Babe — _____

   _____

   Boned out — _____

   _____

   Fly — _____

   _____

   Ends — _____

   _____

   Home boy — _____

   _____

   Peace Cut— _____

   _____

2. Check your definitions with others in your peer group.

3. Ask your trainer to share definitions he or she has.

4. Develop a list of words used by different cultures in your community.

Words	Definitions
_____	_____
_____	_____
_____	_____
_____	_____
_____	_____
_____	_____
_____	_____
_____	_____
_____	_____
_____	_____
_____	_____

HOMEWORK

1. Listen as other people talk and make a list of words that they use with meanings that seem to be unique to their culture. Those same words may have different meanings to other people in your community. If so, note the difference.

2. Study Exercise 5.6 and come prepared to do it during the next group meeting.

RATING THE HELPER

Beginning with this exercise, you will practice and receive feedback (information on how one or more other persons saw you do) on each of the basic communication skills.

During the practice sessions you will work with two other persons. In this triad each person will serve as helper, helpee, and rater.

As you practice, another member of your cluster (small group of two to four people) will give you feedback on the quality of your response when you serve in the role as helper.

You will rate others in your cluster as they serve as helpers. The following ratings are to be used for feedback to the helper. The ratings will be recorded on a Rating Flow Sheet.

GOAL

In this exercise you will learn how to evaluate the quality of attending skills in verbal and nonverbal behaviors.

RATING SCALE FOR ATTENDING BEHAVIORS

The terms High, Medium, and Low will be used to identify the quality of the helpee's attending behaviors. The following statements are definitions of high, medium, and low levels of attending behaviors.

High (H) Response: Helper looked at helpee, looked interested, posture was good, leaned forward with square shoulders, voice tone good, and had eye contact, each of which was present all of the time.

Medium (M) Response: Helper exhibited high attending behaviors at least part of the time.

Low (L) Response: Helper did not exhibit high attending behavior and seldom, if ever, looked at the helpee.

ATTENDING SKILL: RATING FLOW SHEET

DIRECTIONS

1. Helpee presents a problem to which the helper responds.

2. Make three helpee/helper interchanges for one problem.

3. Rate each helper's response.

> Example: Person A (Helpee) states a concern. Person B (Helper) responds by using attending skills. The rater (Person C) will check High, Medium, or Low on the flow sheet for each helper response. The rater then gives feedback.

4. Change roles so that all members of a cluster can be helpee, helper, and rater.

RATING FLOW SHEET

HELPER RESPONSE

1. Helper Number 1 Responses

	High	Medium	Low
Response #1	_____	_____	_____
Response #2	_____	_____	_____
Response #3	_____	_____	_____

2. Helper Number 2 Responses

	High	Medium	Low
Response #1	_____	_____	_____
Response #2	_____	_____	_____
Response #3	_____	_____	_____

3. Helper Number 3 Responses

	High	Medium	Low
Response #1	_____	_____	_____
Response #2	_____	_____	_____
Response #3	_____	_____	_____

HOMEWORK

Study Exercise 5.7 and complete Directions 1 and 2 before the next group meeting.

Name _____

Date _____ Hour _____

SENSITIVITY TO ATTENDING TO PEOPLE OF OTHER CULTURES

In certain cultures eye contact, physical closeness, and touch may be inappropriate. It is important to understand attending mannerisms in different cultures so that you may provide appropriate attending behavior for the helpee.

GOAL

In this exercise you will become better aware of appropriate ways to attend to others.

DIRECTIONS

1. Identify and list other races, cultures, and ethnic groups in this community.

2. Observe appropriate attending in each culture you identified.

3. Discuss with your training group other possible attending skills.

HOMEWORK

1. Think about and write how different cultures will impact your attending skills. Include
   a. How you will attend differently to people of other cultures.

   b. How you will attend differently to people of different ages:
      Elementary children,
      Teens,
      Adults, and
      Elderly people.

   _____

   _____

   _____

   _____

   _____

   _____

   _____

   _____

2. Read the introduction to Module VI.

3. Complete Exercise 6.1 before the next group meeting.

MODULE VI

Empathy

The Second Skill in Peer Helping

8
7
6
5
4
3
2 Empathizing
1 Attending

MODULE **VI**

EMPATHY SKILL

The basic communication skill that you are going to learn in this module is called empathy. This word sounds much like sympathy, and both words have to do with how people relate to each other, but they are very different in their effect. ***Empathy means understanding other individuals so completely that their surface feelings and even their deeper feelings, thoughts, and motives are easily comprehended.*** Sympathy means having pity or sorrow for the distress of other persons. For the most part, empathy assists individuals to grow; sympathy causes individuals to feel hopeless and belittled. Empathy is a word that we use when we are hearing or understanding another person. Empathy involves crawling inside other individuals and seeing the world through their eyes. Empathy involves experiencing the world of other individuals as if you were they. This module is concerned with teaching empathy and ways in which you can identify and communicate empathic responses when in a helping relationship with others.

Empathy is the most significant ingredient in relating with individuals generally, but it is vital when you are in the role of a helper. Research has shown over and over again that the quality of empathy is central to any theory that proposes to help people. When talking about empathy, many researchers use in their theories words such as warmth, compassion, and understanding or words that have similar meanings. The words are used to communicate understanding feelings, thoughts, and motives of others. The ability to understand others' feelings is crucial to helper effectiveness. Research has shown that the ability to communicate empathy is teachable and that most people, through effective training, can learn to be more empathic. Really effective listening skill must be learned. We are not born with this skill. We have plenty of evidence for this in the frequency of misunderstanding between human beings. And yet with some people we feel that we're on the same wavelength.

As with all skills some individuals are better than others with the same or similar skill-building experiences. The same will be true with empathy training. Some trainees will be better at learning and using these skills than others, but this does not mean that those who master the skills more quickly are better persons than those who don't do as well. Whatever level of skill you reach will help you in your relationships with others, and it will help you to understand yourself better.

Because empathizing is a skill that you can learn, it can be taught in the same way that other skills, such as playing the piano, playing football, and skating are taught—one step at a time. Therefore in this module as well as others, the skill will be introduced gradually so that you can master one part of it before proceeding to the next part. When you are asked to do a simple task that seems mechanical, understand that these tasks are the basic fundamental behaviors that need to be learned to develop the skill of communicating understanding (empathy). The nine exercises within this Empathy Skill Module are composed of the basic ingredients of empathy, and when put together they will enable you to respond smoothly and accurately to feelings of others. As your empathy skill is developed, individuals will want to talk to you about their problems more frequently. An additional benefit of training is that you will feel better about yourself. You will tend to become more effective and stronger in your relationships with others.

Several steps are involved in the teaching of empathy, and each needs to be learned in sequence before skills related to empathy can be mastered. Empathy includes discrimination and response. ***Discrimination*** is the ability to separate effective and facilitative empathic communication from ineffective and/or destructive responses. ***Response*** is feeding back accurately the feelings and meanings. The first session in this module will concern your ability to hear well enough that which individuals are saying to repeat it word for word. In this way helpees know for certain that you have heard them. To repeat helpees' statements word for word would be ridiculous, so the next step once word-for-word repetitions have been mastered is to respond by saying accurately what the helpee has said but in your own words. *This process is called paraphrasing and requires the ability to feed back to the helpees an accurate understanding of their feelings and/or meanings.* When paraphrasing is done well, you begin to understand how other persons feel about their situation, and that understanding is communicated to them. As you practice hearing accurately feelings and meanings of their statements and are able to paraphrase these feelings back to helpees, a more complete understanding of their concerns will take place. This new understanding is an expression of accurate empathy.

How can individuals be helped by repeating or paraphrasing in response to what they have said? In the first place, by ***paraphrasing*** you will be telling helpees that you are listening to them well enough to understand their feelings. This does not mean that you simply parrot back what they have said. This relationship in itself is so unusual that it imparts good feelings to the persons with the concern. Secondly, when individuals' own thoughts and feelings are fed back to them, those thoughts and feelings sound different, and this difference increases individuals' understanding of the way they feel. So empathic helper responses enable helpees to get a more complete picture or understanding of their feelings. When you increase the understanding of a problem you increase your ability to deal with it more effectively. For this reason the ability to empathize with others is more helpful initially than any other response. The basis of all effective helping is empathy, and empathy is the foundation of other skills that you will be learning later in your training. When you master the empathy skill, you will have progressed a long way toward being an effective helper.

Use: This skill can be learned effectively by all ages, and we find that youth find it easier to learn "responding to feeling" than do older individuals. For that reason we have spent some time teaching skills of listening for feelings. The empathy skill is one of the most effective skills in helping other persons. The skill can be used with peers listening to other peers, friends who are in a crisis, support groups, small groups, and tutoring.

Name _____

Date _____ Hour _____

DISCRIMINATING AND RESPONDING BY PARAPHRASING

In this exercise you are to practice responding by paraphrasing. As a helper when you use paraphrasing, you attempt to

1. check your own listening to make sure you as helper heard the right meaning,

2. focus on the exact meaning of the helpee (Realize that some people, at times, will have difficulty in mastering the "content" of what is said which is necessary before understanding the meaning.),

3. convey to the helpee that you are trying to understand what he/she is saying, and

4. enable the helpee to know he/she is understood.

Paraphrasing helps concentrate on the content of the message being sent. Basically, the helper attempts to feed back to the helpee the essence of what the helpee has just said. Paraphrasing helps clarify confusing content, brings together a number of comments, and highlights issues by stating them more simply.

An illustration of a statement by a helpee and a paraphrased response by the helper is as follows:

Helpee: "I really don't know where to start."

Helper: "You don't quite know how to begin."

GOALS

In this exercise you will learn

1. empathic behavior through the use of discrimination and communication,

2. the skill of perceiving the meanings of what is said and feelings expressed by peers,

3. to communicate accurately feelings and understanding,

4. to rate the helper's ability in paraphrasing words and to rate paraphrasing behaviors, and

5. to paraphrase the helpee's concerns without changing the meanings of those concerns as expressed and felt by the helpee.

DIRECTIONS

For each of the following helpee statements write a paraphrasing response that is illustrative of how you as a helper might respond.

HELPEE STATEMENTS

1. Helpee: "I don't know what to do; sometimes she is nice and sometimes she is mean."

    Helper: _____

    _____

    _____

2. Helpee: "I am really having a hard time getting my parents to trust me, and it makes me angry every time I go out."

    Helper: _____

    _____

    _____

Name _____

Date _____ Hour _____

RATING SCALE FOR PARAPHRASING

The terms High, Medium, and Low will be used to identify the level of the helper's paraphrasing. The following responses are definitions of high, medium, and low paraphrase.

High (H) Response: The helper accurately hears the words expressed by the helpee. Helpee acknowledges that the content heard was correct.

Medium (M) Response: The helper partially hears the content of the statement.

Low (L) Response: The helper does not hear what the helpee has said.

EXAMPLES OF RESPONSES

Helpee: "I am so tired of getting up every morning and doing what I have to do.

    High (H) Response: "Getting up every morning and going really tires you."

    Medium (M) Response: "You don't like getting up in the morning."

    Low (L) Response: "Do you have your own room?"

DIRECTIONS

1. Form clusters of three when directed to do so by trainer.

2. As the helpee, state a concern to the helper who will restate the verbal message in his/her own words. (Do not try to go beyond the meaning of the actual spoken words.)

3. As the helpee, acknowledge whether or not the content of the concern was correctly understood.

4. As the rater, take brief notes during the helpee/helper interchange to facilitate rating and feedback effectiveness.

5. As the rater, rate responses High, Medium, or Low.

6. As the rater, give feedback to the helper.

7. Change roles so that everyone has an opportunity to be rater, helper, and helpee.

8. As the rater, record helpee statement and helper response, if time allows.

9. As the rater, encircle your rating and comment on your reason for the rating.

ROLE-PLAY WITH FEEDBACK

1. Helpee Statement: _____

   _____

   Helper Response: _____

   _____

       Rating: ___High   ___Medium   ___Low

       Comment: _____

   _____

2. Helpee Statement: _____

   _____

   Helper Response: _____

   _____

       Rating: ___High   ___Medium   ___Low

       Comment: _____

   _____

3. Helpee Statement: _____

   _____

   Helper Response: _____

   _____

       Rating: ___High   ___Medium   ___Low

       Comment: _____

   _____

HOMEWORK

Before the next group meeting read and complete Exercise 6.2.

Exercise 6.2

Name _____

Date _____ Hour _____

FEELING WORDS

To capture other individuals' feelings we need to know many feeling words. We need to develop a "feeling" word vocabulary. We must be able to communicate to helpees an understanding of their feelings.

GOALS

In this exercise you will learn

1. feeling words, and

2. an increase in your own awareness of feeling words.

DIRECTIONS

1. Please read the list of feeling words (affective adjectives). This list of adjectives was developed to help the user find the most appropriate description of perceived feelings. No attempt has been made to organize these words in terms of their degree of intensity.

FEELING WORDS

Happy Feelings	Feelings of Sadness	Feelings of Anger	Feelings of Fear
calm	alone	aggravated	crazy
confident	anxious	aggressive	envious
content	bored	angry	paranoid
curious	detached	annoyed	resistant
ecstatic	disappointed	disgusted	scared
focused	discouraged	frustrated	shocked
interested	exhausted	furious	shy
loved	helpless	hurt	skeptical
playful	indifferent	impatient	surprised
proud	lonely	jealous	terrified
relaxed	miserable	mean	worried
	numb	mischievous	
		resentful	
		torn	

---

2. Respond to the following two situations.

Practice formulating responses to situations. Formulate two responses to each of the following situations.

EXAMPLE

Helpee: "I just don't know which way to go."

Helper: "You feel confused."
          "You feel lost."

a. Helpee: "I feel like I'm being pulled both ways."

    Helper: "You feel _____

    _____"

    "You feel _____

    _____"

b. Helpee: "I am so happy about my A!"

    Helper: "You feel _____

    _____"

    "You feel _____

    _____"

Note that by preceding the adjective with appropriate adverbs you can control the intensity of the communication. For example:

You can feel somewhat angry toward someone. You can feel quite angry toward someone. You can feel very angry toward someone. You can feel extremely angry toward someone.

HOMEWORK

Complete Exercise 6.3 before the next group meeting.

Name _____

Date _____ Hour _____

RESPONDING TO FEELINGS

Suggested behaviors to assist you in listening for feelings are as follows:

1. Listen for all the words that express feelings. This action is important if you are to hear all of the meaning.

2. Time your comments. You don't have to reply to every statement.

3. Paraphrase feeling words and meaning.

GOALS

In this exercise you will learn

1. to understand, as a helper, what the helpee is experiencing; and

2. to communicate to the helpee that "I am with you" and "can accurately sense your feelings."

DIRECTIONS

For each of the following helpee statements write a response that would be illustrative of what you could say to help the person know you listened and heard the feeling expressed.

HELPEE STATEMENTS AND RESPONSES

Example--Helpee: "I really don't know what to do."

Helper: "You feel confused about what to do."

1. Helpee: "I am really uncertain about what to do next year."

Helper: _____

_____

2. Helpee: "It is frustrating when I can't do my math."

Helper: _____

_____

3. Helpee: "My friend makes me mad when he/she makes fun of me."

Helper: _____

_____

HOMEWORK

1. Record five statements you have heard made by others which express feelings.

2. Following each statement, write the response you, as helper, would make to that statement.

3. Be prepared to discuss your responses and why.

4. Read and complete Exercise 6.4 before the next group meeting.

FEELINGS AND EMOTIONS

Levels of emotions can be expressed by different words with similar meanings. Varying degrees of emotion can be expressed by words. Many words of emotions have similar meanings.

GOALS

In this exercise you will learn

1. the process of using similar words for expressing feelings, and

2. to associate meanings with words to be used in paraphrasing ideas.

DIRECTIONS

1. For the words underlined, in the chart titled "Levels of Emotions," compare the levels of emotions expressed by the words listed with similar meanings to the underlined words.

2. Mark the degrees of emotion expressed by each word on the scale of six levels from "less strong" to "strong."

3. For some underlined words, add additional words that express similar meanings and then mark the level of emotion on the scale.

LEVELS OF EMOTIONS

	Level of Comparison					
	Less Strong					Strong
Word	1	2	3	4	5	6

Angry

Mad	___	___	___	___	___	___
Unhappy	___	___	___	___	___	___
Upset	___	___	___	___	___	___
Furious	___	___	___	___	___	___
Irate	___	___	___	___	___	___
Irritated	___	___	___	___	___	___

Unhappy

Down ___ ___ ___ ___ ___ ___
Sad ___ ___ ___ ___ ___ ___
Depressed ___ ___ ___ ___ ___ ___

_____ ___ ___ ___ ___ ___ ___

_____ ___ ___ ___ ___ ___ ___

Happy

Excited ___ ___ ___ ___ ___ ___
Exuberant ___ ___ ___ ___ ___ ___
High ___ ___ ___ ___ ___ ___
Good ___ ___ ___ ___ ___ ___
Great ___ ___ ___ ___ ___ ___
Super ___ ___ ___ ___ ___ ___

Pressure

Squeezed ___ ___ ___ ___ ___ ___
Nervous ___ ___ ___ ___ ___ ___
Caught between ___ ___ ___ ___ ___ ___
Anxious ___ ___ ___ ___ ___ ___

Confusion

Wondering ___ ___ ___ ___ ___ ___
Thinking ___ ___ ___ ___ ___ ___
Mixed up ___ ___ ___ ___ ___ ___

_____ ___ ___ ___ ___ ___ ___

_____ ___ ___ ___ ___ ___ ___

Tense

_____ ___ ___ ___ ___ ___ ___

_____ ___ ___ ___ ___ ___ ___

_____ ___ ___ ___ ___ ___ ___

HOMEWORK

Read and complete Exercise 6.5 before the next group meeting.

Name _____

Date _____ Hour _____

DESCRIBING FEELINGS

This exercise will help you to accumulate and categorize words to use in describing emotions so that you will be accurate in hearing the feelings of another. To be an effective helper, you must be accurate in understanding feelings and spontaneous in responding. This skill involves practice.

Feelings can be in two categories—those that are obvious (surface feelings) and those that are underlying (hidden feelings) or not disclosed by the helpee. To be effective the helper must respond accurately to the hidden feelings of the helpee. At the same time, the helper must be aware of the helpee's surface feelings.

GOALS

In this exercise you will learn

1. to recognize that statements by the helpee often have both hidden and surface feelings present.

2. to respond spontaneously and accurately to the hidden and surface feelings of the helpee.

EXAMPLE

The following is an example of a statement and the feelings present in the statement.

Friend talking to a friend: "I am so mad at myself. It seems like every time I try to do the right thing, I just mess up. It is so hard and frustrating to keep trying."

Surface feelings present: mad, angry, frustrated, defeated, upset.

Hidden feelings present: self pity, feelings of low self-worth, lack of confidence.

DIRECTIONS

1. For Situations 1 and 2 below, please write on your list as many words as possible that the helpee might be feeling.

2. For Situations 3 and 4, please write both surface feelings and hidden feelings for each statement.

3. Refer to your list of feelings and emotions distributed by the trainer.

4. Be prepared to discuss in the group.

SITUATIONS

Situation 1—Teenager talking to a possible employer:

"I was over here yesterday and the day before for an interview about your opening as a waitress, and you weren't here either time. I made an appointment both times, and I don't understand why we can't get together. It makes me feel that without even talking to me you don't want to hire me."

Surface Feelings: _____

_____

Situation 2—Parent to teenager:

"I am really upset when you don't let me know where you are and then you don't come home until 2 o'clock in the morning. Since you have started driving, I worry about car accidents."

Surface Feelings: _____

_____

Situation 3—Student to teacher:

"I realize that I am making an 'F' in your course, but I am really trying hard in the class. Every night I spend a long time trying to figure out how to do the work. It seems like the harder I try, the lower my grades are. What do you suggest I do?"

Surface Feelings: _____

_____

Hidden Feelings: _____

_____

Situation 4—Friend to friend:

"Sometimes I think about quitting work. It seems like I'm always tired and never have time for fun. It's hard going to school and working. I wonder if I could get along without the money."

Surface Feelings: _____

_____

Hidden Feelings: _____

_____

HOMEWORK

Read Exercise 6.6 and come prepared to discuss it at the next group meeting.

Exercise 6.6

PARAPHRASING FEELINGS: RATING THE HELPER

The job of raters is to give constructive information and to provide feedback to helpers. The rater's job is to help helpers to become aware of their communication behaviors. Some characteristics of a helpful rater are

1. focus feedback on behavior rather than on the person. Refer to what the helpers do rather than on what you, the rater, imagine that they do;

2. focus feedback on observations rather than on inferences (Observation refers to what you can see or hear in the behavior of other persons, while inference refers to interpretations and conclusions that you make from what you see and hear);

3. focus feedback on what is said rather than on what is not said; and

4. rate only those skills taught by the trainer.

GOALS

In this exercise you will learn

1. to rate accurately the helpers' ability to paraphrase feelings;

2. to give helpful information to helpers and to learn to provide accurate feedback to help them become aware of communication behaviors;

3. to put into words feelings expressed, to rate those behaviors, and then, assuming the role of a helpee, to portray the feelings; and

4. to complete the Rating Flow Sheet by assuming each of the three roles—rater, helper, and helpee.

RATING SCALE FOR PARAPHRASING FEELINGS

The terms High, Medium, and Low will be used to identify the level of the helper's paraphrasing of feelings and conditions.

High (H) Response: The helper accurately responds to the feelings expressed by the helpee.

Medium (M) Response: The helper responds to the feelings but not with the same degree of intensity as the helpee expressed.

Low (L) Response: The helper does not respond to the feelings of the helpee.

DIRECTIONS

1. Please read the list of feeling words and then practice formulating at least two ways of responding to a situation.

2. Work together as three trainees fulfilling the roles of helpee, helper, and rater.

3. As the helpee, make a statement concerning something about which you as a helpee feel strongly.

4. As a helper, put into words what the helpee seems to have been feeling as often as is necessary for the helpee to acknowledge that the feelings were understood correctly.

5. Look for nonverbal clues such as physical gestures, voice inflections, hesitations, or emphasis on certain words that identify feelings of the helpee in addition to the words that the helpee uses.

6. As the rater, rate the response of the helper using high, medium, or low.

7. As the rater, give feedback to the helper following each of the helper's comments.

8. Change roles so that everyone has the opportunity to be rater, helper, and helpee.

EXAMPLE

Helpee: "I'm getting so tired of getting up every morning and going to school."

Helper (High Response): "You feel annoyed." (Accurately expressed feeling.)

Helper (Medium Response*): "You really feel very angry." (Missed accurate level of feeling.)

Helper (Low Response*): "Getting up for school every morning is boring." (Missed feeling entirely.)

Note: These helper responses might be somewhat how the helpee feels and may keep the conversation going, but if the helper responds with a high response, then the helpee may respond in the following manner:

Helpee: "You're right. I'm so annoyed about who I have to be around that I feel like not going.

Helper (High Response): "You feel like just giving up!" (Notice how different the helpee's last statement was from the initial statement of the helper.)

PARAPHRASING FEELINGS: RATING FLOW SHEET

A. Helpee Statement: _____

_____

Helper First Response: _____

_____

Rating: ____High   ____Medium   ____Low

Comments: _____

_____

Helper Second Response: _____

_____

Rating: ____High   ____Medium   ____Low

Comments: _____

_____

B. Helpee Statement: _____

_____

Helper First Response: _____

_____

Rating: _____High   _____Medium   _____Low

Comments: _____

_____

Helper Second Response: _____

_____

Rating: _____High   _____Medium   _____Low

Comments: _____

_____

HOMEWORK

Read Exercise 6.7 before the next group meeting.

Name _____

Date _____ Hour _____

RATING THE HELPER ON ATTENDING AND EMPATHY

You have practiced both attending and empathy (paraphrasing feeling and meaning) skills and now are ready to be rated on how well you as a helper can combine these two skills. You can learn in two ways how to be more efficient in these two skills by (1) observing and rating another helper and (2) by serving as a helper and being rated by another person.

GOALS

In this exercise you will learn to rate the helper on attending and empathy (paraphrasing, feelings, and meaning).

DIRECTIONS

1. Move into triads upon being instructed to do so by the trainer.

2. Rate the helper on attending and empathic behavior using the same rating scale as in Exercise 5.6 for rating attending behavior.

3. Phrase your response to fit the following format:
   Helper Response: "You feel (Insert feeling word or words.)
   because (State condition or meaning for feeling.)"

4. Change roles until everyone has been rater, helper, and helpee.

5. In rating the helper for each response, consider the three separate parts that constitute the empathic response:

   Feeling Words

   Paraphrasing

   Attending Behaviors

6. As the helper, respond to three helpee statements in a sequence before discussing the ratings.

7. Make alternate statement-response, interchanges between helper and helpee, until the helper has responded three times. Start with the helpee stating a concern.

8. As the helper, respond by paraphrasing feelings and meaning accurately.

9. As the rater, write the feeling word used by the helper and rate the responses for accuracy of feeling and meaning. The rater will give feedback to the helper. Use the Rating Flow Sheet to record your ratings.

10   Change roles until everyone has been rater, helper, and helpee.

11.   Be prepared to discuss your ratings.

RATING SCALE FOR EMPATHIC RESPONSE

The following are rating scales of High, Medium, and Low levels of helper response for empathy:

*Rate **High** (H) if the helper:*   identified feelings using accurate feeling words.

paraphrased accurately what was spoken.

attended by using body languages, gestures, and nonverbal cues that showed interest.

*Rate **Medium** (M) if the helper:*   identified feelings but not too accurately.

paraphrased but without the full meaning coming through.

showed interest in a minimal amount of nonverbal cues.

*Rate **Low** (L) if the helper:*   did not identify feelings.

did not paraphrase.

showed little interest through nonverbal cues.

PARAPHRASING EMPATHY AND ATTENDING
RATING FLOW SHEET

**For Ratings circle H for High,
M for Medium, and L for Low**

Response Number	Write In Feeling Word	Empathy		Attending
		Feeling	Paraphrase Meaning	
1.	_____	H M L	H M L	H M L
2.	_____	H M L	H M L	H M L
3.	_____	H M L	H M L	H M L
1.	_____	H M L	H M L	H M L
2.	_____	H M L	H M L	H M L
3.	_____	H M L	H M L	H M L
1.	_____	H M L	H M L	H M L
2.	_____	H M L	H M L	H M L
3.	_____	H M L	H M L	H M L
1.	_____	H M L	H M L	H M L
2.	_____	H M L	H M L	H M L
3.	_____	H M L	H M L	H M L
1.	_____	H M L	H M L	H M L
2.	_____	H M L	H M L	H M L
3.	_____	H M L	H M L	H M L
1.	_____	H M L	H M L	H M L
2.	_____	H M L	H M L	H M L
3.	_____	H M L	H M L	H M L

HOMEWORK

Read and complete Exercise 6.8 before the next group meeting.

Exercise 6.8

FACILITATIVE AND NON-FACILITATIVE DIALOGUE

Empathic responses which help the trainee to consider a concern in greater depth would be a "facilitative" response. You as a peer helper will strive to help the helpee with each of your responses to delve into the concern expressed by the helpee.

A response which you make to the helpee which either stops the helpee's probe into a concern or does not prompt the helpee to move to further consideration is a "non-facilitative" response (communication stopper).

Your success as a helper rests with your skill at using facilitative responses. The following exercise will help you analyze your facilitative and non-facilitative responses.

GOALS

In this exercise you will learn

1. to analyze dialogue between helpee and helper as to which responses are facilitative and which are non-facilitative responses (communication stoppers).

2. the different kinds of non-facilitative responses and facilitative responses.

3. to identify the communication stoppers within a dialogue.

DIRECTIONS

1. Read "Dialogue I: Non-Facilitative Helper" (below) to gain a feel for what has occurred between the helper and the helpee. (Do NOT attempt to answer questions or fill in blanks at this time.)

2. Read "Dialogue II: Facilitative Helper" to gain a feel for what has occurred between the helper and helpee.

3. Analyze for yourself the differences between the two dialogues and what the helper was doing differently.

4. Reread Dialogue I and analyze each helper response as to whether the response is facilitative or non-facilitative and in the space provided give a letter which labels the response according to the following. (Note that a response may be used more than once):

Non-facilitative Responses	Facilitative Responses
A. Advising, recommending	L. Attending
B. Diagnosing	M. Empathic responding
C. Directing, ordering	N. Minimum responding
D. Diverting, bypassing	O. Open-ended questions
E. Evaluating, criticizing	P. Paraphrasing words (High Rating)
F. Kidding, teasing	Q. Surface feelings, paraphrased
G. Moralizing, preaching	R. Underlying feelings, paraphrased
H. Persuading, arguing	
I. Praising	
J. Supporting, sympathy	
K. Warning, threatening	

5. Reread Dialogue II and analyze each helper response as was done in Direction 4 and label each helper response according to items in Direction 4.

6. Proceed next to the Directions following Dialogues I and II.

7. Be prepared to discuss your answers at the next group meeting.

DIALOGUE I: NON-FACILITATIVE HELPER

1. Helpee: "Hi, Mr. Thompson."

2. Helper: "Can I help you?"

   Example--Answer ___O___

3. Helpee: "Uh, yeah, I've got a problem with my math class. I thought maybe I could talk to you about that."

4. Helper: "Yeah, I've heard a lot of students are upset with math lately."

   Example--Answer ___J___

5. Helpee: "Everybody's complaining, I'll bet. You just wouldn't believe how bad it is. It is horrible! That's what I wanted to talk to you about. I just don't want to go to class anymore!"

6. Helper: "Why don't you drop the class?" ____

7. Helpee: "I need this class in order to get into science. All my future involves science in some way."

8. Helper: "Why don't you change to another class?" ____

9. Helpee: "I've thought of that but this is the only time this math is offered in the schedule."

10. Helper: "Then you will just have to stay there, won't you?" ____

11. Helpee: "But I just can't go because I get so upset, my stomach hurts all day."

12. Helper: "Well, there are a lot of students doing very well in that class." ____

13. Helpee: "So what! Have you ever been in that class?"

14. Helper: "Well, no. I don't go into classes unless invited by the teacher." ____

15. Helpee: "Well, it's pretty bad."

16. Helper: "Wait until you go to college. You'll appreciate having this experience. I can remember most of the teachers are pretty bad. They don't care if you pass or fail." ____

17. Helpee: "You mean you think it is worse in college?"

18. Helper: "Yes, I think they have the worst teaching anywhere." ____

19. Helpee: "Worse than our school?"

20. Helper: "Yeah." ____

21. Helpee: "Oh, I don't know. I had a brother who went to college once and he liked all of his teachers."

22. Helper: "No kidding! That's hard to believe." ____

23. Helpee: "Yeah, but I also had a friend once who hated college. So I asked him about college, and he thought it was pretty bad."

24. Helper: "Well, I'm not sure what I can do to help you with your math." ____

25. Helpee: "Well, maybe you could talk to the teacher and tell him about how upset I get with math."

26. Helper: "Well, that might help. But, you are not learning to be responsible which you should by now." ____

27. Helpee: "But I can't stand it. The way he looks at me and puts me down."

28. Helper: Silence. ___

29. Helpee: "He doesn't even offer to help individually. He always just keeps going through the book."

30. Helper: "Well, he is supposed to cover the book. If he didn't get through, then some of the students would not be able to handle the next course." ___

31. Helpee: "Well, I understand that but I sure wish he could help me individually. I really need to learn it."

32. Helper: "You said something important. If you want to learn something badly enough, you will go ahead and put up with it. . ." ___

33. Helpee: "Well, sure, I have been but that doesn't make it right. So why don't you talk to him concerning how unfair he is?"

34. Helper: "Well, I'm afraid I can't help you with that." ___

35. Helpee: "Well, O.K. I wish you could."

36. Helper: "Good bye."

37. Helpee: "Bye."

DIALOGUE II: FACILITATIVE HELPER

38. Helpee: "Hi!"

39. Helper: "Can I help you?" ___

40. Helpee: "Yeah, I want to talk to you about a problem with my math class."

41. Helper: "Sure. You say that there is something about your math class which is bothering you." ___

42. Helpee: "Yeah. You know, I have to take the class, but it makes me so upset. I don't want to go anymore."

43. Helper: "You feel caught in a bind. That's hard to take." ___

44. Helpee: "Right, I need this class in order to take the next science class, and it is important that I do well."

45. Helper: "It kind of makes you feel trapped, like there is nothing you can do." ___

46. Helpee: "I do feel trapped, I can't go to another class, because there isn't but one section."

47. Helper: "You feel very helpless because there doesn't seem to be a good choice." ___

48. Helpee: "Yeah, I hate it so, I keep skipping class, but that isn't the answer."

49. Helper: "If you didn't feel so angry, you could go there. . ." ___

50. Helpee: "Yeah, I think so."

51. Helper: ". . . . and really enjoy it." ___

52. Helpee: "Well, I don't know if I would enjoy it, but I could tolerate it. You know how it is when the teacher is all business and doesn't care about the students and the students in the class. . . "

53. Helper: "There are many things that bother you about the class." ___

54. Helpee: "Well, you know. . . .like I go to class and ask the teacher for extra help. . . .and he says I'm on my own. I should pay more attention, and I would understand it. I don't feel like he treats me like a real person."

55. Helper: "You think he gives real impersonal treatment. . .and you don't like feeling as if you're just a number rather than a person." ___

56. Helpee: "Yeah, even if I half-way understand, and we are starting to work, I feel real funny because everyone is working with a friend, and I just have to sit there and watch them and do it by myself."

57. Helper: "You feel isolated and alone when the class begins to work." ___

58. Helpee: "Yeah, I think working math should be fun and working things out with others. . . ."

59. Helper: "You enjoy being with others and working together." ___

60. Helpee: "It seems I should either have a buddy to work with or everyone should be quiet so I could concentrate."

61. Helper: "And you're disappointed because you have neither." ____

62. Helpee: "Yeah, it is a really unhappy time, so I only go when I have to, when he is starting on something new."

63. Helper: "You have to force yourself to go to class, but you would feel better if you had someone to work with." ____

64. Helpee: "Well, I don't know if it would help, but I look around and see everyone with someone and I think that would make it better."

65. Helper: "If only you had a friend, you wouldn't feel so alone." ____

66. Helpee: "It's kind of hard to make friends. I just can't go up and introduce myself."

67. Helper: "You feel uncomfortable and a little pushy if you have to introduce yourself, and you can't make yourself do it." ____

68. Helpee: "Well, I don't like to do that because maybe they wouldn't want to work with me because they already have someone else."

69. Helper: "You're afraid they will turn you down. It is really hard for you. You are not sure what words to use." ____

70. Helpee: "I really don't know what to say or do. I might just say something dumb about the math lesson."

71. Helper: "After they listen, you're afraid there is nothing more that they will say." ____

72. Helpee: "I just don't know how to talk to people very well."

73. Helper: "I'm just wondering if that is something you and I might work on. Meeting people, talking with people. . . ." ____

74. Helpee: "Yeah, I'm really very shy, I wish I could get to know people easier, but I just thought that was how it was. I would like to meet people easier and have more friends."

75. Helper: "You really would like to get to know people easier." ____

76. Helpee: "Do you think there is anything we can do about it?"

77. Helper: "Yes, if you are really interested in changing, then it is possible." ____

78. Helpee: "Yeah, I would like to talk about it."

79. Helper: "O.K., I think I can help you to learn ways to develop new friends. When do you want to start working on it?" ____

80. Helpee: "How about tomorrow before math class?"

81. Helper: "Sure let's plan to get together then." ____

82. Helpee: "O.K."

83. Helper: "Bye."

84. Helpee: "Bye."

ANALYSIS OF DIALOGUES I AND II

DIRECTIONS

1. Individually complete the items and be prepared to discuss your responses within the total group.

2. Return to Dialogue I and underline the stoppers within each helper response.

3. Return to Dialogue II and underline the facilitative words within each helper Dialogue.

4. Compare responses on Dialogue I and II and explain how they are different.

5. What was the real problem as stated in Dialogue I?

_____

_____

6. What was the real problem as stated in Dialogue II?

_____

_____

7. Why was Dialogue II different?

_____

_____

8. What are the roadblocks in Dialogue I?

_____

_____

HOMEWORK

Read and complete Exercise 6.9 before next group meeting.

Name _____

Date _____ Hour _____

CHOOSE THE BEST EMPATHIC RESPONSE

GOALS

In this exercise you will learn

1. to identify empathic responses.

2. to select accurately those responses which are empathic responses.

DIRECTIONS

1. In the following situations, select the helper response for each helpee statement that seems to paraphrase accurately the feelings and meaning of the helpee.

2. State why you selected the particular response.

3. Be prepared to discuss in the total group the responses and your reasons for them.

4. Analyze responses in Situations A, B, C, and D so as to answer the following questions:

   a. Was the incorrect response always completely bad?

   b. What characteristics did the correct responses have?

   c. How could you tell the person really understood?

Situation A

Teenager: "I feel so tired all the time. I just don't know what is the matter with me."

Parent Responses: 1. "I'm tired, too. Don't talk to me about being tired. You have no idea."

2. "You feel confused because you are always tired and don't know why."

3. "Probably you haven't been eating all your meals."

Response Chosen: ____ Reason: _____

Situation B

Teenage Girl: "My boyfriend keeps putting me down. I wish I could get him to treat me differently."

Friends' Responses: 1. "Your boyfriend bothers you because he keeps putting you down and you wish he would be different."

2. "Don't worry, my boyfriend does the same thing."

3. "If he puts you down, you should find a different boyfriend."

Response Chosen: ___ Reason: _____

Situation C

Worker: "That guy really gave me a hard time. I was so mad I could hardly keep my mouth closed."

Employer Responses: 1. "You were so angry at that guy, it was difficult to keep quiet."

2. "You know you are here to please the customer."

3. "The best thing to do is just walk away from him and smile."

Response Chosen: ___ Reason: _____

Situation D

Retired Worker: "I'm so bored, it seems like no one cares about me anymore."

Friend's Responses: 1. "You feel like no one cares about you any more or pays attention to you."

2. "Get busy and meet new people!"

3. "That's not true, everyone cares about you."

Response Chosen: ___ Reason: _____

HOMEWORK

Read the introduction to Module VII and come prepared to discuss Exercise 7.1 at the next group meeting.

MODULE VII

Summarizing

The Third Skill in Peer Helping

8
7
6
5
4
3 Summarizing
2 Empathizing
1 Attending

SUMMARIZING SKILL

You as the helper should now be very skilled in attending and empathy skills. These skills alone will communicate to the people you help that you understand them and are interested in listening to them.

People with problems often want more feedback from the helper. They want more input to help them see the problem clearer or from a different angle. ***The skill of summarizing involves listening completely to the person's own concern and then summarizing the problem by giving new light to the helpee.*** You as the helper will add additional dimensions of awareness to the problem. Often when someone else summarizes our problem to us, it is like a light going on. Suddenly we understand and see the concern differently.

To be able to summarize another's problem effectively, you must be very attentive to the helpee. You must capture the important thoughts and feelings expressed in the extended interchange and be able to feed back to the helpee the most important parts of some new insights.

Use: This module can be used with youth (age 12 or above), and adults.

Name _____

Date _____ Hour _____

SUMMARIZING: RATING THE HELPER'S RESPONSES

The summarizing responses by the helper moves the helpee into deeper understanding of his/her problem by summarizing everything that has been stated by the helpee to the helper. Examples of a stem for a helper's summarizing response might be as follows:

1. "What I hear you saying is . . ."

2. "It seems to me that what you're saying is . . ."

3. "The real meaning behind what you're saying is . . ."

4. "The real meaning behind what you're feeling is . . ."

GOALS

In this exercise you will learn

1. to recognize the effectiveness of a summarizing response.

2. to rate the helper in summarizing responses.

RATING SCALE FOR SUMMARIZING RESPONSES

The terms High, Medium, and Low will be used to identify the levels of the helper's summarizing responses to the helpee's statements. Each rating of a summarizing response will be rated according to the following characteristics.

Rate the summary High (H) if

1. The helpee goes on to a deeper understanding of his/her problem.

2. The summary accurately summarizes the feelings and meanings of the helpee's prior statements.

3. The helpee develops a different way of looking at the problem.

Rate the summary Medium (M) if

1. The helper summarizes part but not all of what the helpee has said.

2. he helpee continues to explore the problem.

Rate the summary Low (L) if

1. The summary detracts the helpee from the problem.

2. The helper does not summarize any of the previous interchanges.

RATING FLOW SHEET FOR SUMMARIZING RESPONSES
(Flow Sheets are provided later in this exercise.)

DIRECTIONS

1. Study the example of extended dialogue and summarizing responses.

2. Study the Rating Scale for Summarizing Responses and be prepared to use it.

3. Divide into clusters of three when requested to do so by the trainer.

4. Decide among the three cluster members who will have each of the three roles—helper, helpee, or rater.

5. Conduct in each cluster an interchange which will have at least six helpee-helper response sets.

6. Begin the interchange with the helpee stating a real concern.

7. As helper, summarize the various aspects of the helpee's problem in one summarizing response after about six or eight interchange helpee-helper sets.

8. Request assistance from the trainer when needed.

9. As rater, write on the Rating Flow Sheet the feeling word(s) used by the helper in the interchange and rate the responses for accuracy of feeling and meaning. For specifics on Rating Scale for Paraphrasing Feelings, refer to Exercise 6.6.

10. As rater, rate the quality of the summarizing response (Rating Scale for Summarizing Responses is on previous page) and the helper's attending behavior during the interchange. For specifics on Rating Scale for Attending Behaviors, refer to Exercise 5.6.

11. As rater, write your summarizing response in the space provided if you wish to give a summary different from that of the helper.

12. As rater, give feedback and your reasons for the rating (in the small clusters).

13. Change roles until each member takes the role of helper, helpee, and rater.

EXAMPLE of extended dialogue and summarizing responses

1. Helpee: "I'm really fed up with Mr. Smith."

2. Helper: "You're angry at your teacher."

3. Helpee: "Yes, he tells me if I don't want to work, I don't have to, then he gets mad if I don't work."

4. Helper: "You're upset because the teacher says one thing and does another."

5. Helpee: "He is always on my back. He says I have the freedom to decide but then goes back on his word. It is just like my boss who says he is going to give me more hours if I go back to school."

6. Helper: "You're irritated at your teacher and boss for not following through on what they say."

7. Helpee: "Yes, and my mom is always on my back about school. Push! Push! Push!"

8. Helper: "Your mom gives you a 'hassle' about school and that is hard to accept."

9. Helpee: "It is like everyone tells me what to do, and they don't care what I want to do."

10. Helper: "Like you're not considered in the process and that bothers you."

11. Helpee: "Boy, I would really like to quit school, but I know I need the diploma to get a good job."

12. Helper: "You are really tired of school and feel like giving up."

13. Helpee: "Yeah."

14. Helper summarizing response: "It seems to me that what you're saying is that you are tired of your teacher and boss telling you one thing and doing another. Your mom has really been on you and the combination of all this makes you feel like quitting."

HOMEWORK

Complete Exercise 7.2 before the next training session.

Exercise 7.1 (Continued)

1. **Flow Sheet for Summarizing Responses.**

Helper Response	Empathy Feeling Word	Rating			Summarizing Response	Rating			Attending	Rating		
		H	L	M		H	L	M		H	M	L

2. Write your summarizing response if you wish to give a summary different from that provided by the helper. If none, so state.

_____

_____

3. Reason for giving a different summarizing response.

_____

_____

Name _____

Date _____ Hour _____

USING YOUR NEW SKILLS
YOUR DIARY

You have learned and practiced three basic communication skills—attending, empathy, summarizing. You are now ready to become aware of using three skills with others with whom you associate in your everyday life. You will help them with their concerns, some of which will be simple and others very complex. Regardless of the level of complexity, some or all three of these basic communication skills will be used in helping each person approach his/her concern. Review the previous discussion and exercises before attempting this exercise.

GOAL

In this exercise you will learn to identify and record for a week the skills you have used with the people you have helped.

DIRECTIONS

1. Keep a diary (space provided within this Exercise) about four people you have helped this week.

2. List the appropriate skills you used with each person.

3. Write comments to illustrate your activities or concerns relating to each skill used.

4. Write answers to the two questions asked at the end of the Exercise and be prepared to discuss your responses in either a cluster of your peers or in the total group.

EXERCISE EXAMPLE

Person Helped ____Jim Smith_____ Date ____Monday, Nov. 8_____

Describe Condition
  or Situation _____He was concerned about a date for this weekend._____

Skills Used   Comments Regarding Activities or Concerns Relating To Each Skill Used

Attending _____Squared, Eye contact, Leaned forward_____

Empathy _____Very pleased with how I listened_____

Summarizing _____Summarized on three different occasions_____

Diary for Person Number 1

Person Helped _____ Date _____

Describe Condition
   or Situation   _____

_____

_____

_____

_____

_____

Skills Used   Comments Regarding Activities or Concerns
                                 Relating to Each Skill Used

_____   _____

_____   _____

_____   _____

_____   _____

_____   _____

_____   _____

_____   _____

Name _____

Date _____ Hour _____

Diary for Person Number 2

Person Helped _____ Date _____

Describe Condition
or Situation   _____

                     _____

                     _____

                     _____

                     _____

                     _____

Skills Used   Comments Regarding Activities or Concerns
                                      Relating to Each Skill Used

_____   _____

_____   _____

_____   _____

_____   _____

_____   _____

_____   _____

_____   _____

Diary for Person Number 3

Person Helped _____ Date _____

Describe Condition
   or Situation   _____

_____

_____

_____

_____

_____

Skills Used   Comments Regarding Activities or Concerns
                                   Relating to Each Skill Used

_____   _____

_____   _____

_____   _____

_____   _____

_____   _____

_____   _____

_____   _____

Diary for Person Number 4

Person Helped _____ Date _____

Describe Condition
  or Situation   _____

                      _____

                      _____

                      _____

                      _____

Skills Used	Comments Regarding Activities or Concerns Relating to Each Skill Used
_____	_____
_____	_____
_____	_____
_____	_____
_____	_____
_____	_____

<u>Questions</u>

How are your helping skills with a friend who has a problem different now than before you started in the peer helping program?

_____

_____

What are your feelings concerning your new helping skills?

_____

_____

Other comments, if any regarding your progress in the Peer Helper Training Program.

_____

_____

_____

_____

HOMEWORK

Complete Exercise 8.1 and review Exercise 8.2 before the next training sessions.

MODULE VIII

Questioning

The Fourth Skill in Peer Helping

8
7
6
5
4 Questioning
3 Summarizing
2 Empathizing
1 Attending

QUESTIONING SKILL

Questioning! Questioning! Questioning! One of the easiest things in the world to do in a relationship is to ask questions. Sometimes questioning is good, sometimes it is very poor. Being asked questions can make you feel as if you were receiving the "third degree," which can result in anger and resentment. Asking questions also can be the start of a relationship, it can maintain one, or it may create the feeling of care and concern between people. If you wish to be an effective peer helper, you must avoid some kinds of questions and learn others. One must be able to tell the difference.

Our questions often reveal more than we intend. For example, if we ask questions requiring only short answers and rapid responses, we are fairly manipulative even though this might not be our intent. *One important goal of improving questioning techniques is to manipulate individuals less so that they have more opportunity to be open, creative, and willing to share.*

The most manipulative types of questions are those that can be answered yes or no. This type of questions is not always bad. For example, "Do you wish to have milk for lunch" calls for a simple, direct reply, requiring little thinking. What is bad, however, is to have this type of question dominate our way of communicating. For the sake of your own questioning growth, try to eliminate questions that can be answered yes or no in your conversation. You have probably used them in your communication for years. Considerable effort and practice are necessary to erase these old habits and replace them with new ones. Be assured that if you try to do so, you can find few yes or no types of questions that cannot be revised into new ones encouraging more freedom for the listener.

One of the most natural forms of communication is questioning. Questions can *request important information or they can demand a response from others.* Well-formed questions can start a conversation easily, and when the conversation lags they can invite continuation in a meaningful manner.

Module VIII will focus on teaching effects that questioning has on others and how to ask questions so that you

- help the other person to become more open to you,
- help get information without seeming to demand it,
- help facilitate the relationship so that you can help the other person,
- help maintain conversation, and
- help to start a conversation that will be continued by the other person.

Asking effective questions is a significant skill in peer helper training because, although we all know how to ask questions, we often make mistakes with them. Knowing when to ask questions and how to pose them effectively is an important skill for peer helpers.

Use: This module is more appropriate for persons of high school age or older.

OPEN INVITATIONS TO TALK
(Open-ended Questions)

An open-ended question encourages the helpee to explore himself/herself and the concern held. Through use of the open-ended question, the helper also communicates a willingness to assist the helpee in the exploration.

Open-ended questions help

1. begin a conversation.
2. get the helpee to tell more about a point. "Could you tell me more about that?"
3. give examples to help the helpee understand better. "What do you do when you get angry?"
4. focus on feelings of the helpee. "How do you feel about your math class?"

Closed questions often emphasize factual content as opposed to feelings, demonstrate a lack of interest in what the helpee has to say, and frequently keep him/her in place. Closed questions can be answered by a few words or with a yes or no.

GOAL

In this exercise you will learn to use questioning effectively to keep the interchange ongoing between the helpee and yourself.

EXAMPLES

The following examples contain a comparison of open-ended and closed questions. In each example the content of the question is approximately the same but the structure (i.e., open-ended or closed question) will elicit different responses.

1. Open-ended: "Could you tell me a little about your English Class?"

   Closed: "Do you attend English class?"

2. Open-ended: "How did you feel about English class?"

   Closed: "Do you like English class?"

3. Open-ended: "How do you feel about the time you spent on doing the test?"

   Closed: "How long did it take you to finish the test?"

4. Open-ended: "What did you like about the test?"

   Closed: "Did you like the test?"

Open-ended questions can be used for different purposes. The following examples contain a comparison of open-ended and closed questions for the four purposes listed.

1. Questions which <u>begin a conversation</u>.

    Closed question

    Helper: "Did you go sailing today?"

    Helpee: "Yes."

    Open-ended question.

    Helper: "You look tired, what have you been doing today?"

    Helpee: "Yeah, I feel tired because I have been sailing all afternoon, and it really wears you out."

2. Questions which <u>elaborate on a point by requesting information</u>.

    Closed question

    Helper: "Why did you do it that way?"

    Helpee: "I don't know."

    Open-ended question

    Helper: "I need to know more about what caused you to react that way so that I can understand the problem better."

    Helpee: "Well, I was really frightened and felt that if I didn't act aggressively that you would reject my ideas."

3. Questions which <u>give examples to help the helpee understand his/her behavior better</u>.

    Closed question

    Helper: "Do you throw things when you get mad?"

    Helpee: "No."

Open-ended question

    Helper: "Could you tell me what you do when you get angry?"

    Helpee: "Depends on where I am. Maybe I walk away and maybe I yell at them."

4.   Questions which <u>focus on feelings of the helpee</u>.

    Closed question

        Helper: "Do you get embarrassed when people make fun of you?"

        Helpee: "Yes."

    Open-ended question
        Helper: "You have very strong anxieties about that. Can you identify them more clearly?"

        Helpee: "I seem to get anxious only when I feel that person is angry at me or something I am doing."

DIRECTIONS

1.   Write in the space provided at least three samples to illustrate the difference between open-ended and closed questions and be prepared to discuss with the group.

2.   Have your three examples to illustrate three of the four purposes for open-ended questions.

3.   Try to write an example of the fourth purpose; thus, write four instead of three examples if you can.

EXERCISE

1. Closed Question: _____

    _____

    Open-ended Question: _____

    _____

2. Closed Question: _____

    _____

    Open-ended Question: _____

    _____

3. Closed Question: _____

    _____

    Open-ended Question: _____

    _____

4. Closed Question: _____

    _____

    Open-ended Question: _____

    _____

HOMEWORK

Read and be prepared to complete Exercise 8.2 in the next meeting.

IDENTIFYING GOOD QUESTIONS

As a helper you need to be able to recognize good open-ended questions. The following exercise will add to your competence in this area.

GOALS

In this exercise you will learn

1. to differentiate between poor and good questions.

2. to begin to determine what makes some questions better than others.

DIRECTIONS

1. Read the questions that follow, keeping in mind those that you think are better than others.

2. After reading them, pause for a few minutes and try to determine what makes some of the questions better than others.

3. Indicate by marking in the appropriate space what you think is the rating of the question in terms of openness.

Exercise 8.2 (Continued)

| | Extent of Openness | | | |
Question	Poor	Fair	Good	Excellent
1. Given these characteristics, what kind of student do you want to become?				
2. Who was Martin Luther King?				
3. What significant thing did you do last year?				
4. Do you want mile for breakfast?				
5. Tell me more about your feelings?				
6. What would happen if ten persons were isolated on an unpopulated island because of a plane crash?				
7. How would you show anger?				
8. How did that. . .make you feel?				
9. Is this art good?				
10. Are there more large than little trees?				

HOMEWORK

Read Exercise 8.3 before the next meeting.

Exercise 8.3

RATING THE HELPER ON QUESTIONING SKILL

As a helper you use many ways to relate to the helpee as illustrated in Exercise 8.1. When learning to be a helper, one of your concerns is keeping a conversation continuing between you and the helpee. You will use open-ended questions which begin a conversation, which emphasize a point by requesting additional information, which offer examples to aid the helpee in understanding his/her behavior and which focus on the feelings of the helpee. Use of the different types of open-ended questioning will enable you as the helper to be more complete in your peer helping.

RATING SCALE FOR OPEN-ENDED QUESTIONS

The following is a guide to rate the helper in his/her use of open-ended questions.

Rate the helper High (H) if

1. the helper started conversations effectively,

2. the helpee was able to elaborate a point,

3. the question helped the helpee understand a point, and

4. the question helped the helpee focus a feeling.

Rate the helper Medium (M) if

1. the helpee was able to elaborate on content,

2. the helpee explained more by giving information, and

3. the question helped the helpee to understand problem to a limited extent.

Rate the helper Low (L) if

1. the helper asked closed questions,

2. the helper wanted just information, and

3. the questions stopped the interchange.

GOALS

In this exercise you will learn

1. to rate the helper's use of open-ended questions,

2. to rate open-ended questions and provide feedback to others about their skills at open-ended questioning, and

3. to associate open-ended questions with feeling words.

DIRECTIONS

1. When instructed to do so by the trainer, form clusters of three trainees with each cluster member choosing one of the roles—helper, helpee, or rater.

2. Within each cluster conduct an interchange sequence which will have at least six helper-helpee response sets.

3. As helpee, initiate the dialogue using a problem you have or one that another person has that you know.

4. As helper during the dialogue, ask at least one open-ended question and summarize the helpee's problem when appropriate.

5. As helper, use open-ended questions, where appropriate, to achieve any of the four purposes—opening conversation, elaborating a point, helping helpee to understand, or focusing on feelings.

6. As rater, rate the open-ended question(s) and where appropriate write in your own open-ended questions to suggest to the helper later.

7. As rater, also write helper behaviors occurring during the dialogue which illustrate other peer helping skills—attending, empathy, and summarizing—and rate each of these according to rating scales learned in previous exercises.

8. Following the dialogue, discuss within the cluster what occurred and use the Rating Flow Sheet completed by the rater as a basis of the discussion among the cluster members.

EXAMPLES OF DIALOGUE USING OPEN-ENDED QUESTIONS AND EMPATHY

1. Helper: "You look upset. What happened to you today?"

2. Helpee: "I am so angry at Mr. Taylor, I don't want to go to work."

3. Helper: "You are so irritated with him you did not want to go to work."

4. Helpee: "Yes, you know how he is always picking on me. Well, today he asked me to shut the window. Then when I got up, he told me to sit down. He is really mixed up."

5. Helper: "You feel he is coming down on you, and no matter what you do it isn't right."

6. Helpee: "Yes, he is always looking for me to mess up so he can write me up. Then I won't bother him. What a drag."

7. Helper: "You feel he is just waiting for you to mess up so he doesn't have to fool with you, and this gets you down."

8. Helpee: "Yes, I really wanted to keep the job, but I just can't get along with him."

9. Helper: "You want to keep the job, but you are confused on how to make it with him."

10. Helpee: "Yes."

11. Helper: "How did you handle the situation today?"

12. Helpee: "Well, I just sat down and started arguing with him like I always do."

13. Helper: "You first tried to do what he asked, then you got so upset, you started arguing with him, and you are still angry with him."

14. Helpee: "Yes, I have got to either quit or do something different or he has to get off my back. . . . but that is impossible."

Exercise 8.3 (Continued)

RATING FLOW SHEET FOR OPEN-ENDED QUESTIONS AND OTHER PEER COUNSELING SKILLS OCCURRING

Helper Response Number	Open-Ended Questioning (Check Kind Used) A. Open Conversation B. Elaborate a Point C. Help Understand D. Focus on Feelings				Skill Rating			Attending Skill Behaviors and Rating (HML)	Empathy Skill Behaviors and Rating (HML)	Summarizing Skill and Rating (HML)
	A	B	C	D	H	M	L			
1										
2										
3										
4										
5										
6										
7										
8										
9										
10										
11										
12										
13										
14										

Comments for Rater _____

HOMEWORK

Do Exercise 8.4 and submit it to the trainer.

Exercise 8.4

Name _____

Date _____ Hour _____

DIARY

GOAL

In this exercise you will learn to keep a record (diary) of your questioning skills in helping a friend during the week.

DIRECTIONS

1. Keep a diary this week of questions you ask a friend during the time you are helping that friend.

2. Determine if the questions are open-ended or closed. Refer to Exercise 8.3 for Rating Scales of High, Medium, or Low for open-ended questions.

3. Be prepared to discuss your diary at the next training session.

4. Be prepared to discuss how open-ended questions have helped your interchanges.

5. After completing the diary on the next page, write the answers to the following questions in the space provided and be prepared to discuss items with the other trainees and the trainer in the next training session.

EXERCISE

1. What is the difference between open-ended questions and closed questions?

_____

_____

_____

_____

2. Prior to helping friends this week, record some open-ended questions you might use in an interchange.

_____

_____

_____

_____

Diary of Questions Used While Helping Friends With a Problem During the Week

Person With Problem	Open Conversation		Elaborate Point		Help Understand		Focus on Feelings	
	Open-ended	Closed	Open-ended	Closed	Open-ended	Closed	Open-ended	Closed
Name								
Date								
Name								
Date								
Name								
Date								

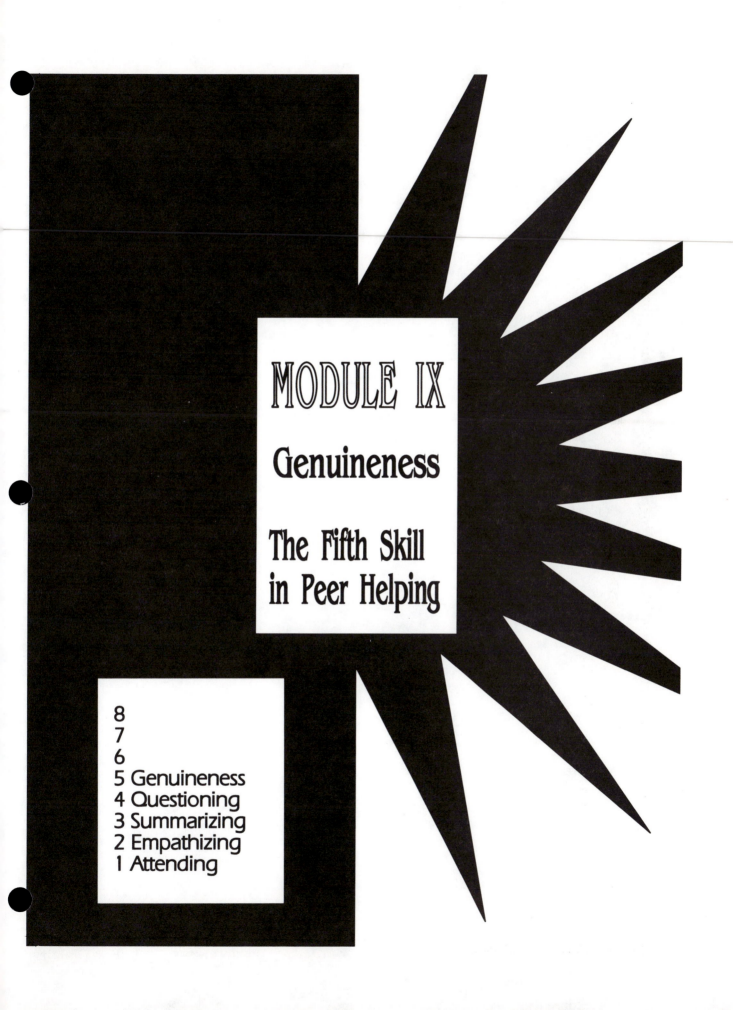

MODULE IX

Genuineness

The Fifth Skill in Peer Helping

8
7
6
5 Genuineness
4 Questioning
3 Summarizing
2 Empathizing
1 Attending

GENUINENESS SKILL

Skills you have practiced previously have been designed to get other people to communicate more and explore their problems or concerns more deeply. When acting as helpers, we may develop feelings about what the helpee is saying or doing. The helper can learn to express these real feelings in such a way as to maintain the relationship.

As you interact daily with people, you may at times feel strongly about their actions or words. Sometimes you may feel your rights as an individual have been violated and on other occasions individuals will irritate you. When people have strong feelings about others' behaviors, they usually choose either to say nothing or become aggressive. This aggression often takes the form of verbal or physical attack. By withdrawing in these situations you end up feeling hurt and angry at yourself for keeping your feelings pent-up. On the other hand if you become aggressive, you anger or hurt others. When you withdraw, the other person does not change his/her behavior and when you attack, you may lose a friend.

By learning to be genuine you can learn to express your feelings about others' behaviors in such a way as to maintain the relationship and increase the chance that others will change the behavior that disturbs you. Genuine interchanges frequently lead to a better understanding between two people and improve the chance that the conflict can be resolved with each having input toward the solution.

To learn the genuineness skill, you must be willing to understand and accurately express your real feelings to others. This expression is called being open or genuine. In this module the trainer will take you through some experiences to help you find out how open and genuine you are. If you can learn to be genuine, assertiveness and confrontation will be easy to learn.

The genuineness skill will enable you to express your genuine feelings in ways that will help the relationship to improve. The trainer will take you through step-by-step processes so that you can learn effective genuineness skill. Your trainer also will help you to implement your skills so that they can be used in helping relationships. Learning the effective genuineness skill will enable you to be a better helper; it also will enable you to become stronger and better in your everyday relationships.

One goal of the module on genuineness skill will be to learn to share feelings about what the other person is saying or doing, and maintain and enhance the relationship at the same time. You will be able to express your feelings at the end of this module rather than concealing your feelings. Your own attitude about openness will be examined and you will be assisted to share more of your feelings. You also will learn how to integrate with genuineness your earlier skills of attending, empathy, and questioning.

Use: The genuineness skill is best used with high school students and adults. It can be used as a separate exercise in working with shy people as well and as an introduction to the assertiveness skill or as an introduction to working with couples and families.

Name _____

Date _____ Hour _____

A COMPARISON OF NONRESPONSIVE, NONGENUINE, AND GENUINE RESPONSES

Our responses to another person can be examined in terms of how open or genuine we are. In this exercise, we will examine responses of three kinds:

1. <u>nonresponsive</u> in which the person making the response is emotionally dishonest or indirect.

2. <u>nongenuine</u> in which the response may be emotionally honest but is made at the expense of the other person, and

3. <u>genuine</u> in which the person responds with emotional honesty and directly expresses own feelings.

GOALS

In this exercise you will learn

1. to differentiate among the three kinds of responses as to nonresponsive, nongenuine, and genuine.

2. differences in the feelings of a person making each of the three kinds of responses and what feelings each of the responses generally cause in the person to whom the response is made.

DIRECTIONS

1. Read the example and study the differences in the three kinds of responses.

2. Write responses to each of the four situations that would be illustrative of the three kinds of responses.

3. Review the Chart of Feelings to help yourself understand what feelings you and the other person may have during the behavior.

4. Be prepared to discuss your responses with the group.

EXAMPLE

In the following example are listed different ways of responding to a statement that bothers you.

Situation: After listening to a friend criticize, cut down, and call someone else names that you care about, you respond by

1. Nonresponsive: "You are right about my friend." Or ". . . . ." (Silence, say nothing.)

2. Nongenuine: "You are always cutting down other people; why don't you look at yourself first?"

3. Genuine: "I feel very uncomfortable when you cut down my friend, and it causes me to try and change the subject when you start cutting my friend down."

CHART

The chart on the next page will enable you to identify the level of genuineness (non-phoniness) in the way you respond to others when you can identify feelings you have toward them. You may use the chart to help you understand difference in feelings to be expressed as you write responses for this exercise.

Exercise 9.1 (Continued)

Name ———————

Date ——————— Hour ———————

CHART OF FEELINGS DURING THREE KINDS OF RESPONSE BEHAVIORS

General Behavioral Characteristics →	Characteristics of Your Behavior	Your Feelings During the Behavior	Other Person's Feelings About His/Her Self When You Are Doing Behavior Which Results From That Behavior	Other Person's Feelings Toward You As A Result Of Your Behavior
Nonresponsive behavior ↑	Emotionally dis-honest, indirect	Hurt, anxious at times and angry later	Guilty or superior	Irritated, pity, disgusted
Nongenuine behavior ↑	Emotionally honest at expense of	Righteous superior, guilty later	Hurt, humiliated	Angry, vengeful
Genuine behavior ↑	Emotionally honest, directly expressive of feelings	Confident, self-respecting now and at later times	Valued, respected	Generally respect

FOUR SITUATIONS

1. <u>Situation</u>: Another person says to you, "Our friend Alice is getting to be terrible. She constantly does things she shouldn't do and she knows better, too."

Nonresponsive
response: _____

_____

Nongenuine
response: _____

_____

Genuine
response: _____

_____

2. <u>Situation</u>: A friend of yours keeps doing something in your presence that you dislike, such as excessively teasing little children.

Nonresponsive
response: _____

_____

Nongenuine
response: _____

_____

Genuine
    response: _____

_____

---

3. Situation: You are at a public gathering, such as a ball game, and the stranger on the seat beside you keeps doing things that prevent you from seeing and/or hearing the action, for example, holding up a pole with a large banner in front of you each time the major actions start occurring and/or blowing a loud horn during the times the announcer gives information about the game.

Nonresponsive
    response: _____

_____

Nongenuine
    response: _____

_____

Genuine
    response: _____

_____

4. Situation: A helpee with whom you have been talking says to you, "You aren't helping me. You don't know what you are doing."

Nonresponsive
    response: _____

_____

Nongenuine
    response: _____

_____

Genuine
response: _____

_____

HOMEWORK

If Exercise 9.2 is not covered in the same training session as 9.1, then study and complete Exercise 9.2 before next session.

Exercise 9.2

HOW OPEN AM I?

GOALS

In this exercise you will learn

1. to assess kinds of feelings you would discuss with friends and relate these kinds of feelings shared to how close your relationships are to these friends.

2. to recognize how open you are with your own feelings.

DIRECTIONS

1. Think of several topics you might discuss with others.

2. Write each topic under one of the four kinds of persons listed in the exercise.

3. Identify four topics for each kind of person listed.

4. Be prepared to share your responses with the group.

EXERCISE

1. Intimates (Closest friends)

   Example: My fears and ambitions.

   a._____

   b._____

   c._____

   d._____

2. Friends (People with whom I spend time)

   Example: Personal information about myself.

   a._____

   b._____

   c._____

   d._____

3. Acquaintances (People I know casually.)

   a._____

   b._____

   c._____

   d._____

4. Strangers (People you have just met or a person situated next to you in a situation such as on a bus, at a ball game, or in a new group in which you were just placed.)

   a._____

   b._____

   c._____

   d._____

DIRECTIONS

1. Review the topics you wrote that you would discuss and with what kind of people.

2. Complete the rating scale on the degree of your openness, that is consider how completely open (able to talk with anyone about anything) or completely closed (keep all personal topics to self) you are.

3. Mark your behavior with a check mark for each of the four kinds of people and overall.

Exercise 9.2 (Continued)

	Completely Open-ended	Generally Open-ended	Sometimes Open, Sometimes Closed	Generally Closed	Completely Closed
With Intimates					
With Friends					
With Acquaint-ances					
With Strangers					
Overall					

HOMEWORK

Study Exercise 9.3 and come prepared to complete it during the the next group meeting.

Exercise 9.3

Name _____

Date _____ Hour _____

OPENNESS CIRCLE

GOALS

In this exercise you will learn

1. how the more open a person is, the more feelings and experiences that person shares with friends, acquaintances, and strangers.

2. how to examine your own openness level.

DIRECTIONS

1. Be prepared to examine your openness as you and the other trainees perform the exercise.

2. Follow the instructions as given to you by the peer training trainer.

HOMEWORK

Study and complete Exercise 9.4 before the next group meeting.

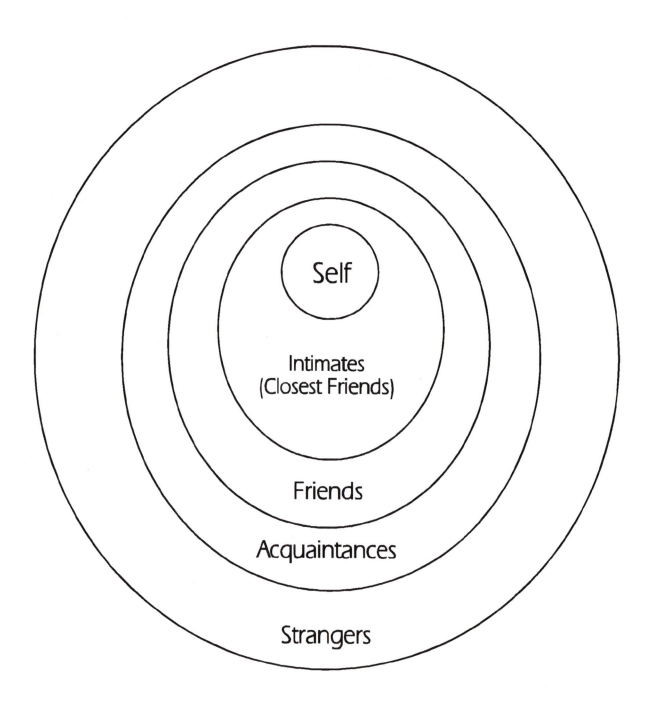

Self

Intimates
(Closest Friends)

Friends

Acquaintances

Strangers

Name _____

Date _____ Hour _____

PUTTING TOGETHER A GENUINE MESSAGE

In learning to be genuine, one sends "I" (genuine) messages as opposed to "you" (nongenuine) messages. "I" (genuine) messages include four parts.

1. Identifying the process of reporting the helper's **feelings** regarding the helpee's behavior.
    Example: *"I feel nervous when. . . ."*

2. The **specific happenings** of the helpee's behavior that affect the helper.
    Example: *"I feel nervous when you yell so frequently."*

3. The **reasons** for the helper's affective reaction to the helpee's behavior.
    Example: "I feel nervous when you yell so frequently *because I get threatened."*

4. *Communicating the* **effects** *on helper's feelings if behavior continues.*
    Example: *"I feel nervous when you yell so frequently because I get threatened, and I want to get away from you."*

GOALS

In this exercise you will learn

1. to make a complete response with a genuine message to a situation.

2. to express how your feelings relate what has happened.

3. to identify the effect on yourself.

4. to explain the reasons for your feelings about and reactions to the situation.

COMMUNICATION MODEL

The communication model for the helper to use in putting together a genuine message is as follows:

I feel __(feeling stated)__ **because** __(what has happened)__
and I __(effect on me)__ **for** __(for the reason that)__ .

DIRECTIONS

1. Study the communication model to be used by helper in putting together a genuine message.

2. Write a genuine message that fits the model and be prepared to read it to others for the purpose of identifying the four parts. Write your genuine message on the next page in space provided in Exercise 1.

3. Examine the examples and study how to record information from the message into the exercise (space provided).

4. Be prepared to complete this exercise (similar to the example) from statements read to you by the trainer.

5. Cluster into groups of two and read to each other your genuine message written as result of Direction Number 2.

6. Identify the four parts in the other cluster member's genuine message and write the four parts into the chart space.

7. Share with each other in your cluster what the four parts of each other's genuine message were.

FORMULATING AND ANALYZING GENUINE MESSAGES

1. In the space below write a genuine message that you might make. Be sure your message fits the communication model.

   Your genuine message: _____

   _____

   _____

2. In the following chart, on the next page, record the four parts of the genuine message recorded in Number 1 (An example is provided in the chart).

Name _____

Date _____ Hour _____

	How I Feel	What Has Happened	How This Affects Me (This is sometimes hard to say, but do so whenever you can.)	Reasons
Example:	nervous	yell	want to get away	get threatened
Trainer's Prepared Genuine Message				
Other Cluster Member's Statement				

3. In the second space under heading "Other Cluster Member's Statement" write the four parts as instructed in Direction Number 6.

HOMEWORK

Study and complete Exercise 9.5 before the next group training.

Exercise 9.5

Name _____

Date _____ Hour _____

WHEN TO USE A GENUINE MESSAGE

The purpose of genuineness is to respond honestly and openly to feelings expressed by another person. Use genuine messages when another person

1. creates a situation that causes a problem with you.

2. is inclined to give advice, criticize, or preach, and you may become upset.

Use a genuine message when you

1. have been using good listening and now want or need to tell what's going on inside you.

2. have an experience or feeling that you want to share.

GOALS

In this exercise you will learn

1. to respond genuinely by using role-play situations.

2. to report accurately with a genuine message on how this role-played situation makes you feel.

DIRECTIONS

1. Choose a partner whose role is to confront you with a situation that will create some kind of feeling in you.

2. Role-play situations with your partner using the example situations listed in the Exercise section under "Situations to be Role-Played." Your partner will confront you with the situation.

3. Report genuinely how you respond at the feeling level to his/her behavior.

4. Change roles and role-play the situations so that both of you have the experience in responding with genuine messages.

5. Share with each other how you feel about the experience.

SITUATIONS TO ROLE-PLAY

Situations to be role-played (The first four are for youth, the last three are for adults.)

In Youth Training Groups:

1. Your friend has been changing gradually. The clothes he/she wears have been "way out." You have noticed that you are becoming embarrassed when you go places with him/her. (Youth)

2. You have a new friend. Today, you found him/her flirting with your steady. (Youth)

3. You are taking a test. Your classmate keeps trying to read your answers over your shoulder. (Youth)

4. Your mother cooked a meal which included some of your favorite foods. (Youth)

In Adult Training Groups:

5. You've been out of touch with your friend for a while. You've really missed him/her. . .but you've been busy. Now you go to the store to get some things, and you run across him/her at the store. (Adult)

6. A co-worker has promised to complete a project so that you can do your job. (Adult)

7. You are worried about your team because they won't study or be responsible. (Adult)

HOMEWORK

Study and complete Exercise 9.6 before the next group meeting.

Name _____

Date _____ Hour _____

PRACTICE SENDING GENUINE RESPONSES

GOAL

In this exercise you will learn to write a genuine message for a given situation as a contrast to a nongenuine message already prepared.

DIRECTIONS

1. Read sample situations supplied and prepare a genuine message for each situation before going to the next situation.

2. Read the nongenuine message for each situation.

3. Write a genuine message for each situation.

4. Be prepared to discuss your responses in the group.

SITUATIONS

1. Situation: Your friend forgot to be on time to a movie and you are to have the car back at a certain time which is shortly after the first movie is over. (Youth)

   Nongenuine
   Message: "You should be ashamed. After all, I agreed to go to the movie, and now you're late."

   Genuine
   Message: _____

   _____

   _____

2. Situation: Your parents keep bugging you about keeping your room clean and it is hard to do since you share it with a brother/sister. (Youth)

   Nongenuine
   Message: "Mom, you really don't understand how hard it is to keep a room clean with him/her there, too."

Genuine
Message: _____

_____

_____

3. Situation: A friend has been avoiding you for the last few days, and you don't
know the reason. (Youth)

Nongenuine
Message: "Come on, now. Stop avoiding me. Either tell me why you're mad at
me, or just forget our friendship."

Genuine
Message: _____

_____

_____

4. Situation: A coworker has not talked to you all week, and you don't know the
reason. (Adult)

Nongenuine
Message: "If you don't want to talk to me, then I can be the same way."

Genuine
Message: _____

_____

_____

UNDERSTANDING HOW GENUINENESS IS USED

Genuineness in helpers' responses is appropriate in a helping situation. Understanding how genuineness is used is the major purpose of this exercise. You will be able to examine the dialogue between the helpee and the helper and to gain an understanding of what peer helping skill is used by the helper and how the response makes a difference to the helpee.

Before a helper can respond genuinely, the helpee must make one or more statements that generate feelings in the helper toward the helpee. The dialogue example identifies an effective response pattern between helpee and helper when the helper is responding with empathy and genuineness. The pattern of back and forth dialogue shows the helper responds alternately with empathy and genuineness depending upon which skill seems appropriate as a response. By studying the dialogue you will be able to understand how the process functions.

GOALS

In this exercise you will learn

1. to identify when genuineness is appropriate for a situation.

2. to rate the genuineness of response and the level of genuineness.

3. to rate empathic and genuine responses.

RATING SCALE FOR GENUINENESS RESPONSES

When you function as a rater and are rating genuineness responses of the helper, you will find the following rating scale helpful. You will use a rating system similar to that used previously in your training. You will rate high for high levels of the condition rated, medium for conditions that contain part but not all of the conditions necessary to be rated as high, and low for responses that do not reveal the characteristics of the skill being rated. The following rating scale will help you identify high, medium, and low conditions of genuineness.

High (H):   Rate high if the genuineness responses included all four of the conditions of genuineness listed below:

1. TRUE FEELINGS of sender—How I really feel.

2. SPECIFIC HAPPENINGS—What happened to create these feelings?

3. REASONS—Why do I react as I do?

4. EFFECTS—How I will react if the conditions continue to exist.

Medium (M): Rate medium if the response contains two or three of the items listed previously.

Low (L): Rate low if one or none of the items listed previously are used.

EXAMPLE of Genuineness Response for Each Rating Scale

High Genuineness Response

"I'm really disappointed in you for not paying me back the $5.00 or letting me know when you would pay me back and that makes me very hesitant to ever loan you money again."

Medium Genuineness Response

"I'm really disappointed in you for not paying me back the five dollars."

Low Genuineness Response

"Hey, do you remember I loaned you five dollars?"

EXAMPLE of Dialogue in which Empathy and Genuineness Responses are used.

Helpee's Statement No. 1: "Jim, I just got paid for last week and I don't know whether to put it in savings or put it on a down payment for that stereo I've been wanting."

Helper's Response No. 1: "You're really feeling puzzled as to how to use that paycheck." (Empathy) "I get angry when you want me to help you solve the problem because you haven't paid me the ten dollars you have been owing me for six weeks." (Genuineness)

Helpee's Statement No. 2: "Man I feel horrible I completely forgot about that and I'm glad you reminded me. You just solved part of my problem; I will make that O.K. tomorrow."

Helper's Response No. 2: "My telling you that really caused you to feel bad. That wasn't what I meant to do but I am glad that you want to straighten it out."

EXAMPLE of Rating Flow Sheet for Empathy and Attending Behavior

Helper's Response Number	Empathy Response and the Rating				Attending Behavior			
	Feeling Words	H	M	L		H	M	L
#1	You're really feeling puzzled	X				X		
#2	Caused you to fee badly	X				X		

EXAMPLE of Rating Flow Sheet for Genuineness ("I" Messages) Behavior

Helper's Response Number	Feelings	Specific Happening	Effects	Rating on Genuineness		
				H	M	L
#1	Angry	want me . . .	haven't		X	
#2	Glad	(implied not stated)	you want to . . .		X	

EXAMPLE of Dialogue to Illustrate when using Empathic and Genuineness Responses

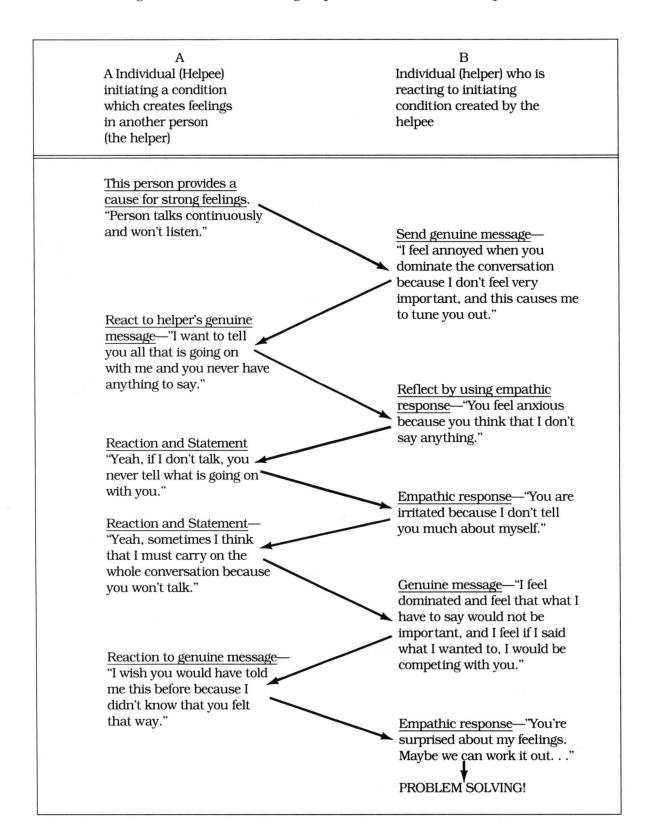

A	B
A Individual (Helpee) initiating a condition which creates feelings in another person (the helper)	Individual (helper) who is reacting to initiating condition created by the helpee

This person provides a cause for strong feelings. "Person talks continuously and won't listen."

Send genuine message— "I feel annoyed when you dominate the conversation because I don't feel very important, and this causes me to tune you out."

React to helper's genuine message—"I want to tell you all that is going on with me and you never have anything to say."

Reflect by using empathic response—"You feel anxious because you think that I don't say anything."

Reaction and Statement "Yeah, if I don't talk, you never tell what is going on with you."

Empathic response—"You are irritated because I don't tell you much about myself."

Reaction and Statement— "Yeah, sometimes I think that I must carry on the whole conversation because you won't talk."

Genuine message—"I feel dominated and feel that what I have to say would not be important, and I feel if I said what I wanted to, I would be competing with you."

Reaction to genuine message— "I wish you would have told me this before because I didn't know that you felt that way."

Empathic response—"You're surprised about my feelings. Maybe we can work it out. . ."

PROBLEM SOLVING!

Name _____

Date _____ Hour _____

DIRECTIONS

1. Divide into clusters of three consisting of helpee, helper, and rater when instructed to do so by trainer.
2. As helper, listen to the helpee when he/she makes statements which create feelings in the helper.
3. As helper, be prepared to role play with the helpee. Recognize that the helper will establish the situation by describing the role function that you are to initiate (behavior that bothers the helper).
4. As helper, respond with genuineness and then listen with empathy. (Refer to example on previous page.)
5. As rater, listen to the empathic and genuineness responses and observe the helper's attending behavior.
6. As rater, use the following form for recording ratings.
7. As rater, give feedback to helper as to quality of responses.
8. Change roles until each member has had an opportunity to be a helper, helpee, and rater.

EXERCISE AND RATING FLOW SHEET

Helper's empathy responses Feeling Words	Rating			Attending Behavior		
	H	M	L	H	M	L

Helper's Genuineness Responses Specific Reasons for Feelings	Feelings	Effect			Rating		
					H	M	L

HOMEWORK

Study and complete Exercise 9.8 before the next group meeting.

Exercise 9.8

Name _____

Date _____ Hour _____

INTEGRATING COMMUNICATION SKILLS

GOALS

In this exercise you will learn

1. to rate responses as to the quality of conditions of attending, empathy, summarizing, questioning, and genuineness.

2. to give feedback on the quality of the helper's skills.

3. to act upon feedback given you.

DIRECTIONS

1. When instructed to do so by trainer, form clusters of three for an extended dialogue in which you will rate each other on five peer helping skills—attending, empathy, summarizing, questioning, and genuineness.

2. Among the three cluster members take the roles of helper, helpee, and rater until you have role-played each role once.

3. As rater, rate all five skills. You are to pay special attention in this exercise to how well the helper responds genuinely when he/she, for some reason, has real feelings toward the helpee that interfere with his/her ability to help. Your responsibility is to rate how genuine the helper,s responses were when these feelings occurred.

4. As helper, respond both with empathy and genuineness and then with empathy again after a genuine response was made.

5. As rater, rate the quality of all five conditions if they apply. Use the previously provided rating scales—for attending see Exercise 5.6; for empathy, Exercise 6.7; for summarizing, Exercise 7.1; for questioning, Exercise 8.3; and for genuineness, Exercise 9.7.

6. As helpee, role-play a situation in which you can interact with the helper in an extended dialogue.

HOMEWORK

Complete Exercise 9.9 and submit it at the next group meeting.

Exercise 9.8 (Continued)

EXAMPLE of Rating Flow Sheet for Integrating Communication Skills

Attending			Empathy Feeling Words	Rating			Summarizing			Questioning			Genuineness (Write-in "I")	Rating		
H	M	L		H	M	L	H	M	L	H	M	L		H	M	L
X			Puzzled	X			Not Applicable			Not Applicable			Expressed Anger		X	
X			Feel Bad			X	X			Not Applicable			Relief and Pleased	X		

EXERCISE AND RATING FLOW SHEET FOR INTEGRATING COMMUNICATION SKILLS (Examples are provided on first two lines)

Attending			Empathy Feeling Words	Rating			Summarizing			Questioning			Genuineness (Write-in "I" Message)	Rating		
H	M	L		H	M	L	H	M	L	H	M	L		H	M	L

HOMEWORK

Complete Exercise 9.9 and submit it at the next group meeting.

Exercise 9.9

Name _____

Date _____ Hour _____

USING GENUINE RESPONSES

GOALS

In this exercise you will learn

1. to record genuine responses.

2. to identify situations in which genuine responses are used.

DIRECTIONS

1. List the situations on the next page in which you responded genuinely since in the last training session. (Become aware that genuineness is not just used in helping situations but many other times in everyday life.)

2. Record responses you made in each situation.

3. Be prepared to discuss your responses in the next training session.

SITUATION	RESPONSE MADE
<u>EXAMPLE</u> A. Teacher accuses me of cheating. B. Boss accuses me of not completing a project on time.	A. "When you accuse me of cheating, I feel hurt because I don't want you to think less of me." B. When you accuse me of not completing the project in time, I am frustrated because I don't know what the due date is so I just guess. Sometimes it is ok, and sometimes it's not.
Your Experience:	Your Response:

(Use extra sheet if needed)

HOMEWORK

Study the introduction to Module X and complete Exercises 10.1 and 10.2 before the next group meeting.

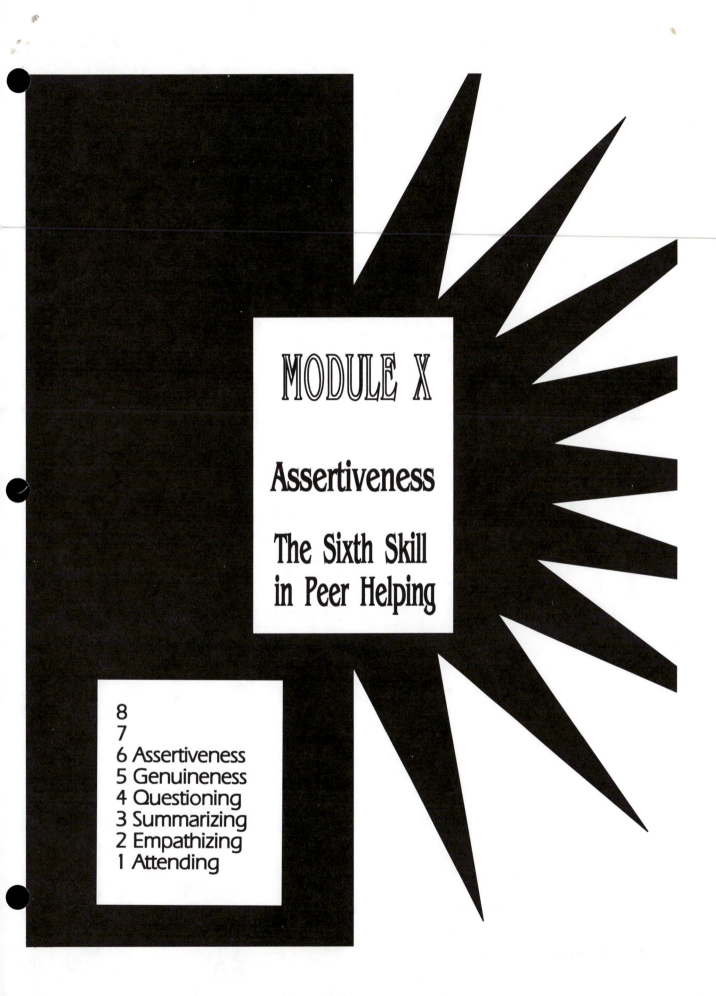

MODULE X

Assertiveness

The Sixth Skill in Peer Helping

8
7
6 Assertiveness
5 Genuineness
4 Questioning
3 Summarizing
2 Empathizing
1 Attending

ASSERTIVENESS SKILL

Many individuals confuse assertion and aggression. To recognize the difference and to use assertion rather than aggression is very important as a helper. Both assertion and aggression involve standing up for one's rights. The crucial difference, however, is that the aggressive person violates the rights of others while the assertive person does not.

EXAMPLES

Situation Number One: At a meeting a young man is distracted by a conversation taking place behind him. He turns around and says hostilely,

Aggressive—"Would you shut up, I can't hear."

Assertive—"I'm having trouble hearing. Would you please stop talking?"

Situation Number Two: When the time comes for evaluation on the new job, the employee is unhappy about receiving a lower evaluation than expected. The employee goes up to the boss and states,

Aggressive—"My work deserves a better rating. Redo my evaluation right now."

Assertive—"I've really worked hard at learning this job, and I think I descrve a higher evaluation. I would appreciate your reconsidering my evaluation.

Many individuals experience unsatisfactory interpersonal relationships and frequently attribute the responsibility for this failure to others. However, a multitude of ways may exist that interfere with individuals' own ability to meet their needs. Assertiveness training is a model that is designed to help the individual deal effectively with this interference.

One crucial assumption of assertion training is that every individual is entitled to certain human rights. Among these rights are dignity, respect, and courtesy. It becomes the responsibility of individuals, however, to stand up for these rights once they become aware of them.

Assertiveness skill enables one to stand up effectively for one's own dignity, respect, and courtesy without violating the rights of others while at the same time helping others to recognize and more completely obtain their rights.

We often end up in situations where we feel that others are taking advantage of us. We at times do not stand up for our rights. The skill of assertiveness is an important skill. The goal of this training module will be to assist you in determining assertive, nonassertive, and aggressive communications, and to be able to recognize your own style of communication. You also will have an opportunity to role play various situations where you may want to learn effective assertiveness skill. This skill is an extension of genuineness and very necessary in learning the skill of confrontation.

Use: This module may be used with high school students or adults. It can be used as a separate training program.

Exercise 10.1

DIFFERENCES AMONG ASSERTIVE, NONASSERTIVE, AND AGGRESSIVE BEHAVIORS

Assertive Behavior

Assertive behavior involves the ability to express thoughts and feelings in an honest, straightforward fashion that shows respect for the other person. Assertive individuals feel good about themselves. They are capable of expressing both positive and negative feelings and opinions and have no need to rely on "not telling the whole truth." They are open, willing to take risks, and are responsible for their own behavior. Rather than relying on fate, good fortune, or other individuals, assertive persons actively engage in meeting their needs.

Behaving in an assertive manner is healthy and satisfying. Assertive individuals are aware of their basic human rights and can stand up for them. They are able to express how they are feeling and what they are thinking in an honest, firm, direct way. They are sensitive to the feeling and rights of others and usually feel good about themselves and their world.

Nonverbal components of assertive behavior include

1. good eye contact,

2. spending time with the other person,

3. calm appearance,

4. facial expression consistent with speech characteristics and content, and

5. good posture.

Verbal components of assertive behavior include

1. expressing feelings and beliefs honestly and directly;

2. standing up for one's legitimate rights;

3. expressing respect and empathy for others;

4. using "I" statements;

5. taking the initiative in interpersonal encounters;

6. offering alternatives; and

7. strong, firm voice.

Acting assertively often involves taking some risk and does not guarantee your getting your own way. It does, however, help you feel good about yourself. It also involves a responsibility to spend time with the other person and work through the issue on both sides.

EXAMPLES

1. "I know you need help on that project, but I'm tied up for the next few weeks and I don't have the time."

2. "I've worked hard in the job and feel strongly that I need a raise. If I don't get one, I'm afraid I'll be very disappointed."

Nonassertive Behavior

Acting nonassertively is an ineffective way of communicating. Individuals who are generally nonassertive have difficulty expressing their opinions, beliefs, and feelings. They do not stand up for their legitimate rights and may feel as though they are taken advantage of by others.

Nonassertive persons inhibit honest, spontaneous reactions and typically feel hurt, anxious, and sometimes angry as a result of their behavior. They frequently send double messages. Verbally they say, "Sure, I'll be glad to babysit," while nonverbally they have a tight mouth, weak voice, and indirectly communicate the opposite message.

Characteristics that nonassertive individuals display include the following:

1. exhibiting shyness;

2. being anxious and nervous;

3. discounting their own worth as persons and make others more important;

4. enjoying martyrdom;

5. placing others' wants and needs ahead of their own;

6. allowing others to make decisions for them;

7. often thinking of what they should have said too late to say it;

8. seldom being able to say no;

9. feeling guilty about saying no;

10. assuming others will know what they need;

11. keeping negative feelings inside (which may result in sadness, stomachache, headaches; and

12. often sending double messages (e.g., saying "It's okay," while tone of voice indicates anger).

Some components of nonassertive behavior are as follows:

1. not stating thoughts and feelings directly,

2. apologizing,

3. making excuses,

4. giving in to requests of others,

5. being silent, and

6. inappropriately agreeing with others.

Aggressive Behavior

Acting aggressively is another ineffective way of communicating. Persons who respond aggressively violate the rights of others. Aggressive persons may think that the only way to get their point across is to yell or cut someone else down.

The purpose of aggressive behavior is to humiliate, dominate, or put the other person down rather than simply to express one's honest emotions or thoughts. It is an attack on the person rather than on that person's behavior.

Aggressive individuals do not feel good about themselves. To make believe that they do feel good about themselves, they put others down in both blatant and subtle ways.

Aggressive persons exhibit a number of characteristics, for example, any or all of the following:

1. inappropriately expressing their feelings and opinions;

2. violating the rights of others;

3. discounting others, often in a sarcastic way, making themselves feel more important;

4. at times, being confrontive, hostile, sarcastic, blaming; and

5. making decisions for others.

Verbal components of aggressive behavior include the following:

1. using "you" rather than "I" statements;

2. using blame and sarcasm;

3. taking no responsibility for own behavior;

4. making no self-disclosing statements;

5. attacking worth of others;

6. demanding own way; and

7. being sarcastic, hostile, or using unusually loud tone of voice.

Nonverbal components of aggressive behavior include the following:

1. glaring or condescending eye contact;

2. tightening facial muscles; and

3. holding body in an attacking or threatening body posture (e.g., hand on hips, leaning forward, finger pointing).

GOALS

In this exercise you will learn

1. differences among assertive, nonassertive, and aggressive behavior; and

2. when to use these different forms of communication.

DIRECTIONS

1. Study the information supplied in the introductory material to Module X.

2. Think of instances when you may be assertive, nonassertive, and aggressive.

3. Think of other individuals whom you know—such as your parents, teachers, employees, and friends—and try to think of instances when they acted in an assertive, nonassertive, or aggressive manner.

INSTANCES

1. Name some instances when you behaved in the following manner, how you felt, and the result of your behavior.

Assertive:

    Instance _____

    _____

    Feelings _____

    _____

    Result _____

    _____

Nonassertive:

    Instance _____

    _____

    Feelings _____

    _____

    Result _____

    _____

Aggressive: _____

_____

Instance _____

_____

Feelings _____

_____

Result _____

_____

2. Name some instances when individuals you know acted in the following manner, how it made you feel, and the results.

	Parent	Teacher	Employer	Other
Assertive:				
Instance				
I felt				
Result				
Nonassertive:				
Instance				
I felt				
Result				
Aggressive:				
Instance				
I felt				
Result				

HOMEWORK

Complete Exercise 10.2 including the Assertiveness Scale before the next group meeting.

Exercise 10.2

Name _____

Date _____ Hour _____

MY ASSERTIVENESS PROFILE

GOALS

In this exercise you will learn

1. to clarify how assertive you are, and

2. to understand in which situations you are assertive.

DIRECTIONS A

1. Circle the numbers in items 1 through 38 on the next two pages that describe your typical behavior.

2. Follow the directions at the end of the questionnaire.

BEHAVIORS

Responses: 3—Usually   2—Sometimes   1—Rarely

		U	S	R
1.	I participate in group activities without fear of being embarrassed.	3	2	1
2.	I make decisions easily.	3	2	1
3.	When a latecomer is served before I am, I object.	3	2	1
4.	I express my feelings.	3	2	1
5.	I am comfortable when someone watches me at work.	3	2	1
6.	If I am unhappy with the food in a restaurant, I send it back.	3	2	1
7.	I avoid being a wallflower in social situations.	3	2	1
8.	I am able to express openly my affections to others.	3	2	1
9.	If a friend makes an unreasonable request I can say no.	3	2	1
10.	I talk louder than normal to get others to agree with me.	3	2	1
11.	I get into physical fights with others.	3	2	1
12.	When persons are being unfair, I call it to their attention.	3	2	1
13.	I control my temper well.	3	2	1
14.	If a person has not returned a borrowed item, I remind them that it is overdue.	3	2	1
15.	If someone keeps kicking my chair, I ask them to stop.	3	2	1
16.	I return damaged merchandise.	3	2	1
17.	I stand up for my own point of view.	3	2	1
18.	When meeting new people, I start the conversation.	3	2	1
19.	I resist sharing test answers with a friend.	3	2	1
20.	I openly criticize the opinions and ideas of others.	3	2	1

21. When someone breaks into line in front of me, I speak up. 3 2 1

22. I have confidence in my own judgment. 3 2 1

23. I insist that other members of my family accept their fair share of household chores. 3 2 1

24. I speak up in a group meeting or debate. 3 2 1

25. I resist sales pressure even though the sales pitch is strong. 3 2 1

26. I continue an argument after another person has concluded the discussion. 3 2 1

27. I maintain eye contact when talking with another person. 3 2 1

28. I avoid name-calling when angry. 3 2 1

29. I ask my friends for help. 3 2 1

30. I think I'm always right. 3 2 1

31. I ask someone to stop smoking if it bothers me. 3 2 1

32. I control group conversations. 3 2 1

33. If I think I have received an unfair grade, I talk to the instructor about. 3 2 1

34. I complete other individuals' sentences for them. 3 2 1

35. It is easy for me to get to class on time. 3 2 1

36. I select a seat with a group in the cafeteria. 3 2 1

37. I feel comfortable talking to a member of the opposite sex. 3 2 1

38. I enjoy reading nonfiction paperbacks. 3 2 1

Your assertiveness behavior score _____
(See Numbers 1 and 2 under Directions B.)

DIRECTIONS B

To indicate your level of assertive behavior complete the following steps:

1. Cross out the following numbers: 5, 10, 11, 17, 20, 21, 26, 34, 35, 38. These are not to be included in your final score because they are not considered to be assertive behaviors.

2. Total your responses for the remaining statements. This is your assertive behavior score.

3. Mark your score on the Assertiveness Scale to find your level of assertiveness ("Almost never," "Sometimes," "Most of the time").

4. Discuss individual results with the other participants and review your own questionnaire to determine the types of activities that affected your total score.

ASSERTIVENESS SCALE

100	Usually assertive
90	
80	
70	
60	
50	Sometimes assertive
40	
30	
20	
10	
0	Rarely assertive

HOMEWORK

Complete Exercise 10.3 before the next group meeting.

Exercise 10.3

Name _____

Date _____ Hour _____

WHEN SHOULD I BE ASSERTIVE?

Step three in assertiveness training is to identify those situations in which you want to be more effective. The questionnaire that you completed previously will help you objectively analyze your own behavior.

GOALS

In this exercise you will learn

1. to identify those situations where you need to be more assertive,

2. to identify those situations that are very threatening to you, and

3. to identify those areas where you may want to make some changes.

DIRECTIONS

1. To refine further your assessment of situations in which you need to be more assertive, complete the Questionnaire to Assess Assertiveness that starts on the next page. Put a check mark in Column I by those items that are applicable to you, and then rate those items in Column II. Use the following scale to record your answer in Column II as to how you feel in relation to your behavior:

   1. comfortable

   2. tolerable

   3. uncomfortable

   4. threatened

   5. unbearable

2. Examine the pattern of your answers, and analyze the pattern for an overall picture of what situations and kinds of individuals threaten you. How do nonassertive and aggressive behaviors contribute to the specific items you checked on the list?

3. In constructing your own program for change, it will be useful to focus initially on items you rated as being either 2 or 3. These are situations that will be easiest to change. Items you rated as 4 or 5 will be more difficult to change.

QUESTIONNAIRE TO ASSESS ASSERTIVENESS

I Check Items Applicable to Self	II Own Behavior Rated from 1 through 5 for Degree of Discomfort	**A. Behaviors I Can Or Do Exhibit**
————	————	Asking for help
————	————	Stating a different opinion
————	————	Listening to and sending negative feelings
————	————	Listening to and sending positive feelings
————	————	Dealing with someone who refuses to cooperate
————	————	Speaking up about something that annoys me
————	————	Talking when all eyes are upon me
————	————	Protesting a rip-off
————	————	Saying "no"
————	————	Responding to undeserved criticism
————	————	Making requests of authority figures
————	————	Negotiating for something that I want
————	————	Having to take charge
————	————	Asking for cooperation
————	————	Proposing an idea
————	————	Taking charge
————	————	Asking questions
————	————	Dealing with attempts by others to make me feel guilty
————	————	Asking for services
————	————	Asking for a date or appointment
————	————	Asking for favors

Name _____

Date _____ Hour _____

B. Interactions With Other People

_____ _____ Parents

_____ _____ Fellow workers

_____ _____ Classmates

_____ _____ Strangers

_____ _____ Old friends

_____ _____ Family members

_____ _____ Girlfriend/boyfriend/spouse

_____ _____ Employer

_____ _____ Children

_____ _____ Acquaintances

_____ _____ Salespeople, clerks, hired help

_____ _____ More than two or three individuals in one group

_____ _____ Other: _____

C. Want And Have Acted To Obtain

_____ _____ Approval from others for things I do well

_____ _____ Some help with certain tasks

_____ _____ More attention from or time with ones I love

_____ _____ To be listened to and understood

_____ _____ More satisfaction from what are or have been boring or frustrating situations

_____ _____ To not have to be nice all the time

_____	_____	Confidence in speaking up when something is important to me
_____	_____	Greater comfort with strangers, store clerks, mechanics, and so on
_____	_____	Getting a new job, asking for interview(s)
_____	_____	Comfort with people who supervise me or work under me
_____	_____	To not feel angry and bitter a lot of the time
_____	_____	To overcome a feeling of helplessness and the sense that nothing ever really changes.

A list of three areas in which I want to make changes.

1. _____

2. _____

3. _____

HOMEWORK

Complete the part of Exercise 10.4 before the next group meeting than can be done outside of the group.

Exercise 10.4

DAILY LOG

The next step is to describe your problem scene. Select from Exercise 10.3 three areas in which you may want to make changes. Be sure to select a tolerable or uncomfortable situation that suggests itself from the items of the Questionnaire to Assess Assertiveness. You will be given homework assignments to keep logs for the next few days. A log is similar to a diary. It should include a written description of interpersonal encounters with your perception of what happened, with whom, how you felt at the time it happened as well as afterwards, and what the consequences were.

GOALS

In this exercise you will learn

1. to identify past scenes in your life and significant aspects of them.

2. to increase your awareness of your behavior and relationships with others.

3. to identify which situations and which individuals are difficult for you to deal with effectively.

EXAMPLES

Following is an example of a poor scene description:

"I have a lot of trouble persuading some of my friends to listen to me for a change. They are consistently talking and there is never enough time for me. It would be nice for me if I could participate more in the conversation. I feel that I'm just letting them take over for me."

Notice that the description ignores

a. the identity of the particular friend—who,

b. times this is a problem—when,

c. the way the person is acting—what,

d. the way you deal with it—how,

e. fears involved in being assertive—fear, and

f. goals for increased involvement in the conversation—goal.

Try again. Here is a better example:

> "My friend Sue [who], when we go out for a hamburger [when], often goes on nonstop about her family problems [what]. I just sit there and try to be interested [how]. If I interrupt her, I'm afraid she'll think I just don't care [fear]. I'd like to be able to change the subject and talk sometimes about my problems with my family [goal]."

DIRECTIONS

1. Write a description of the scenes from Exercise 10.3, being certain to include (a) the identity of the person involved, (b) when it takes place (time and setting), (c) what bothers you about it, (d) how you deal with it, (e) your fear of what will take place if you are assertive, and (f) your goal. Space is provided in this exercise for your description to be written.

   Always be specific. Generalizations will make it difficult later to write a script that will make assertive behavior possible in this situation.

2. Discuss your scenes in the group.

3. Break up in clusters of three and read to your partners the scenes from Exercise 10.3 that you have written and practice role-playing your assertive statement. The third person should give feedback concerning the effectiveness of the assertiveness.

4. Keep a log for the next few days or weeks on scenes in your life. Your group trainer will read your logs and give you thoughtful comments.

5. For your homework assignment, keep a log for the next few days similar to the following sample log:

Name *Janice Smith*

Date *1-13* Hour _____

Description of the Scene:

This morning when I was shopping no one waited on me, so I finally went to a clerk and asked her to help me.

At lunch a friend asked me to take care of her children tomorrow, and I said no. I think she was surprised because I always say yes, but I already had plans.

Last night a friend called and wanted to talk. I was so tired, so I told her I couldn't talk now because I was tired and would call her tomorrow.

HOMEWORK

1. Keep a log as asked by your leader.

2. Study and be prepared for Exercise 10.5 for next group meeting.

Exercise 10.5

ASSERTIVE RIGHTS

To be aware of our assertive rights is often difficult; for many people to practice those rights by saying no and meaning it is even more difficult. Learning assertiveness skill will help overcome those difficulties. This exercise will help you learn to feel more comfortable in saying no.

GOALS

In this exercise you will learn

1. the basic assertive rights, and

2. to say no assertively.

DIRECTIONS

1. Study the Basic Assertive Rights statements (next page) and discuss them.

2. Answer the questions on Basic Assertive Rights.

3. Form into clusters of two each.

4. One member of the cluster plays the role of a persuader who says only "Yes, you will." Ask this person to think back to a time when persuading someone to do something was really important. Ask the person to imagine that it is now important to convince the other person to give in.

5. The other member plays the role of the refuser who says "No, I won't" to the demands of the partner. Ask this person to think back to a time when saying no really meant no and to imagine that it is now that important to say no.

6. Persuader and refuser sit facing each other. The persuader uses a tone of voice that convinces the refuser that the persuader means yes. The refuser looks the persuader in the eye, sounds firm, does not smile, and says "No, I won't."

7. Persuader and refuser exchange roles.

8. Discusses the experience in the total group.

BASIC ASSERTIVE RIGHTS

1. Right to freedom of opinion and expression.
2. Right to be independent.
3. Right to change your mind.
4. Right to say "I don't know."
5. Right to say "I don't understand."
6. Right to say "I don't care."
7. Right to make mistakes.
8. Right to feel and express anger.
9. Right to refuse requests without feeling guilty.
10. Right to offer no excuses to justify your behavior.

QUESTIONS ON BASIC ASSERTIVE RIGHTS

1. Do you agree with these rights?

   _____

2. Should there be additional rights? If so, give examples.

   _____

3. Can these rights be carried too far? If so, illustrate.

   _____

4. If you exercise these rights, what responsibility do you have for the other person?

   _____

5. Are there appropriate times to be assertive? Give illustrations.

   _____

HOMEWORK

1. Continue to keep logs as requested in Exercise 10.4.

2. Before the next group meeting study Exercise 10.6.

Exercise 10.6

PUTTING ASSERTIVENESS SKILLS INTO ACTION

Often much practice is required to learn to be assertive and stand up for yourself. The following is an exercise that will help you practice your skills.

GOALS

In this exercise you will learn

1. to practice assertiveness skills, and

2. to put together assertive messages.

EXAMPLES OF ASSERTIVE STATEMENTS

"I dislike it when you interrupt me halfway through a sentence and would appreciate your not doing it any more."

"I feel rather nauseated by your cigarette smoke. It's bothering me, and I'd appreciate it if you'd put it out."

COMPONENTS OF ASSERTIVE BEHAVIOR

1. **Eye Contact.** Looking directly at a person to whom you are speaking is an effective way of declaring that you are sincere about what you are saying and that your words are directed to that person.

2. **Body Posture.** The weight or import of your messages to others is increased if you face the person, stand or sit appropriately close, lean toward the person, and hold your head erect.

3. **Gestures.** A message accented with appropriate gestures takes on an added emphasis; overenthusiastic gesturing, however, can be distracting.

4. **Facial Expression.** Have you ever seen someone trying to express anger while smiling or laughing? It just does not come across. An effective assertion requires an expression that agrees with the message.

5. **Voice Tone,** Inflection, Volume. A whispered monotone will seldom convince another person that you mean business, while a shouted response may cause the listener's defenses to obstruct the path of communication. A level, well-modulated, conversational statement is convincing without being intimidating.

6. **Timing.** Spontaneous expression generally will be your goal because hesitation may diminish the effect of an assertion. Judgment is necessary, however, to select an appropriate occasion. For example, consider a student who has been distracting other students during a student council report. The teacher might speak to the student alone rather than in front of the class, where he/she may feel the need to respond defensively.

7. **Content.** What you say is important. Expressing yourself by honestly stating your own feelings is more effective than downgrading the other person. You could downgrade the student in the previous example by saying "You really are a jerk!" Or you could assert your point of view by saying "I'm really frustrated that you keep talking when I'm trying to give the report."

DIRECTIONS

1. Look at the specific "Situations To Be Used In Role-Play" and pick one for your triad. One person makes the assertive statement, another person responds, the third person gives the rating using the Rating Flow Sheet for Assertive Messages.

2. Exchange roles and repeat so that each person has played all three roles.

3. If time permits, select a second situation and repeat Directions 1 and 2.

SITUATIONS TO BE USED IN ROLE-PLAY

1. A friend wants to borrow money that you have saved.

2. Your parents ask you to cancel your plans to go out so that you can be with them.

3. A salesperson refuses to fix a defective radio you just bought.

4. Someone complains constantly to you about personal problems.

Name _____

Date _____ Hour _____

RATING FLOW SHEET FOR ASSERTIVE MESSAGES

Circle the rating for each aspect of each situation. Ratings are H (High, good assertion), M (Medium, average assertion), and L (Low, poor, or nonexistent assertion).

ASPECT	Situation 1	Situation 2	Situation 3	Situation 4
Physical Expression				
Body Posture	H M L	H M L	H M L	H M L
Gestures	H M L	H M L	H M L	H M L
Facial Expression	H M L	H M L	H M L	H M L
Eye Contact	H M L	H M L	H M L	H M L
Verbal Expression				
Voice Tone	H M L	H M L	H M L	H M L
"I" statements	H M L	H M L	H M L	H M L
Feelings	H M L	H M L	H M L	H M L
Specific situation	H M L	H M L	H M L	H M L
How it affects me	H M L	H M L	H M L	H M L
My goal	H M L	H M L	H M L	H M L

HOMEWORK

1. Read and study the introduction to Module XI.

2. Study and complete Exercise 11.1 before the next group meeting.

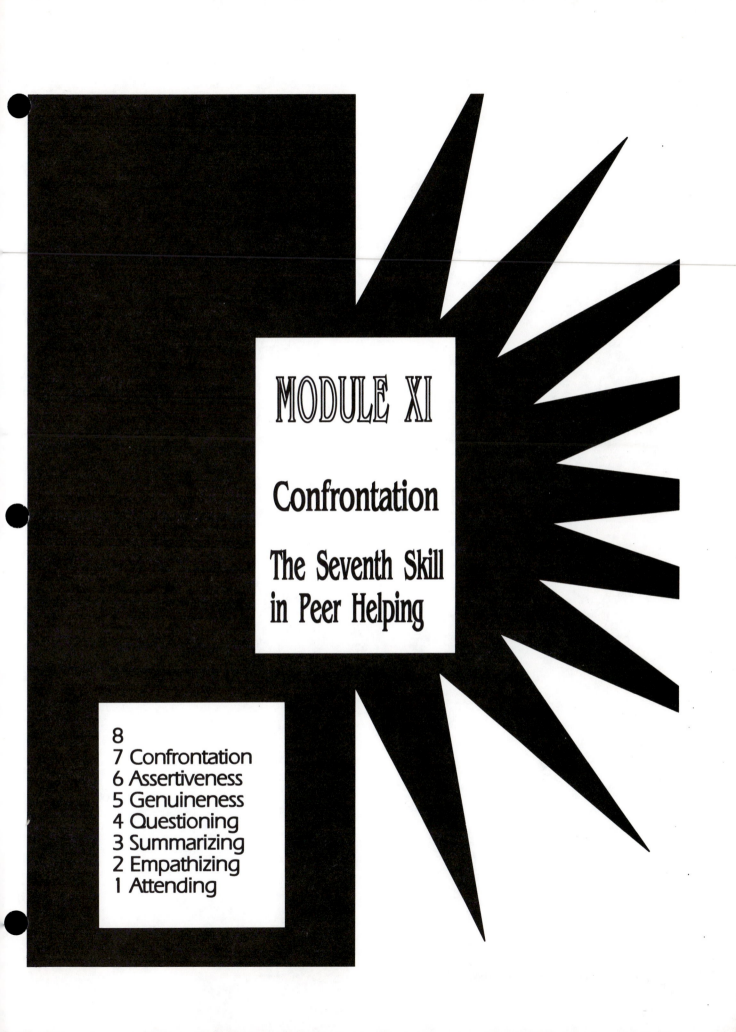

MODULE XI

Confrontation

The Seventh Skill in Peer Helping

8
7 Confrontation
6 Assertiveness
5 Genuineness
4 Questioning
3 Summarizing
2 Empathizing
1 Attending

CONFRONTATION SKILL

We frequently are given conflicting messages that cause us either to disbelieve one of the messages and accept the other or to be confused about which is the accurate message. Friends may tell us that they really want to succeed in getting good grades, but in the very next breath tell us that they never do homework or study for tests. These comments form a double message because they can't both be true. To deal effectively with a double message we use a skill called confrontation. **Confrontation skill is being able to identify and to respond— communicate, provide feedback—regarding those discrepancies in another person's behavior in such a manner that the other person can grow.**

Often, as a peer helper, you are put in a position in which people begin to trust you and tell you one thing, but do another. The skill of confrontation is very helpful in dealing with this situation. For example, someone may promise to quit a self destructive habit but continue the habit on special days such as on the weekend. Confrontation is the appropriate skill for this situation. At times, with your friends or family, you will receive double messages when they may say one thing and do something else. If an intervention is needed, then being able to confront another person often will lead to change in the person's behavior. Role playing and practice situations will be utilized in learning this skill.

Confrontation, when done well, enables us to point out the two messages the other person is expressing without our creating anger or defensive behavior on that person's part. In this way we can make sure, without the risk of losing a friend or acquaintance, that the other person is either aware of the confusion or gives us only one message or changes the message.

Confrontation is one skill that can be used when you decide to level with friends about their conflicting behavior or about something that bothers you. Possibly a friend has been drinking too much lately or has been breaking promises; these are just a few examples of situations in which you may want to use confrontation.

The following material is designed to teach you confrontation skill for your use with people about whom you care.

DEFINITION OF CONFRONTATION SKILL

Confrontation is best described as the means that a helper uses to call attention to differences or discrepancies in such situations as the following:

A. Difference between what the helpee is saying and doing.

     Example: "You say you deserve an A in the course, but at the same time you have been telling me all the things on which you have done poorly in the course.

B. Difference between what the helpee has been saying and what others have reported him/her as having done.

     Example: "You tell me you have been studying one hour after school, but your mother told me that you never study after school hours."

C. Difference between what the helpee says and how he/she feels or looks.

     Example: "You say you are not angry, but your voice sounds upset and your face looks very angry."

CHARACTERISTICS OF CONFRONTATION SKILL

1. The helper must possess an accurate understanding of the helpee and must have used empathy and genuineness.

2. Confrontation is to be timed so that the person being confronted is open to receiving the interpretation without becoming defensive.

3. Confrontation must be related to the situation in which the two people are engaged; it should not appear unexpectedly.

4. Confrontation should be concise and to the point.

5. The confronter must be able to communicate a genuine and sincere interest in the well-being of the person being confronted.

GUIDELINES FOR USE IN CONFRONTATION

1. Confront the person when you are calm and have planned what you are going to say.

2. Have careful documentation for what you are saying. Use examples.

3. Confront the person at a time when and location where others are not present.

4. Time the confrontation so that the person being confronted is open to receiving the interpretation without becoming defensive.

5. Make the confrontation concise and to the point.

6. Communicate a genuine and sincere interest in the well-being of the person being confronted.

7. Give the other person plenty of your listening time.

8. Have someone else sit in on the confrontation if appropriate.

Use: This module can be used with older high school students and adults. It can be a separate training program to be used in drug and alcohol intervention training, for confronting people to receive or to seek professional help, and in employer-to-employee, parent-child, or teacher-student relationships.

Exercise 11.1

CONDITIONS OF CONFRONTATION

The decision to confront another person is made upon two major conditions:

1. the quality of the relationship (generally, the stronger the relationship the more powerful the confrontation may be), and

2. the perceived ability of the person being confronted to act upon the confrontation.

If at the moment a person's anxiety level is high or the person's motivation or ability to change is low, the confrontation will not be utilized as an invitation for self-examination, therefore, it should not take place.

Confrontation is a combination of high empathy and genuineness and must be done so as to help the relationship grow and become more productive. To confront in a blunt, destructive manner is seldom helpful to the relationship or the person being confronted.

Confront another person only if you do intend to get involved with the person and can stay involved with the person. The involvement would need to be the kind where the helper would feel free enough to try genuineness, empathizing, summarizing, and so forth.

The purpose of confrontation is to free the person being confronted so that he/she can engage in better behavior. Therefore, try confrontation when you as a helper believe you can assist the helpee to try new behavior after he/she is aware of this unwanted behavior.

Two conditions that help decide whether to confront the helpee and illustrative questions to ask oneself for determining whether or not each condition is met are as follows:

1. The quality of the relationship.
   Illustrative Question: Do I, the helper, experience a close relationship?

2. The ability of the person being confronted to act upon the confrontation.
   Illustrative Question: Is the person emotionally strong enough to understand the confrontation?

The determination of how strongly you word a confrontation depends on how certain you feel. For example, if you are very aware of the discrepancies of the helpee's behavior, then you will have a strong confrontation.

GOALS

In this exercise you will learn

1. conditions under which confrontation can be helpful.

2. kinds of a relationship you, as helper, need with a helpee for confrontation to be effective in peer helping.

3. how your skills of empathy and genuineness are essential for meaningful confrontation.

EXAMPLE

Person: My best friend Jim.

Quality of Relationship: I have known him for 10 years and we spend much time together.

Incident: Jim got so drunk last night that he threw up on his date and I had to drive him home. This is the sixth time this has happened in the last two weeks.

Confrontation Statement: "I have become increasingly upset at your drinking behavior. Every time we've been together in the last few weeks you have drunk so much that you had to throw up and I had to drive you home. The last time you had such a hangover you made me late for school trying to get you up. Your parents are really worried about your drinking and so is your girlfriend. I'm so upset that I can't continue to hang around with you if you keep on like this. What I want you to do is to get some help for your drinking problem and quit drinking."

DIRECTIONS

1. Study the information supplied

   a. as introductory material to Module XI.

   b. as introduction to this Exercise, 11.1.

2. Think of someone you would feel comfortable confronting.

3. In identifying the person, consider the quality of relationship you have with the person.

4. Identify a behavior or an incident involving the person identified in Direction 2 in which there were differences between what the person says and does or differences between what others say and what the person does.

5. For the behavior or incident identified in Direction Number 4, develop a confrontation statement.

6. Record your responses to Directions 2, 3, 4, and 5 in the spaces provided in the Confrontation Consideration (next section).

7. Be prepared to discuss your responses to Directions 4 and 5 (not 2 and 3) within the group in the next session.

CONFRONTATION CONSIDERATION

1. Identify by name the person you would feel comfortable confronting.

_____

2. Describe the quality of the relationship you have with the person listed.

_____

_____

_____

3. Describe the behavior or incident about which you feel you could confront the person and be helpful to him/her.

_____

_____

_____

_____

4. Develop a confrontation statement appropriate for the behavior or incident described in Number 3.

_____

_____

_____

5. Summarize what you learned from this exercise.

_____

_____

_____

HOMEWORK

Study and complete Exercise 11.2 before the next group meeting.

Name _____

Date _____ Hour _____

PERCEIVING CONFRONTATION SKILL

GOALS

In this exercise you will learn

1. the way confrontation responses can differ in their helping potential, and

2. to rate confrontation responses.

DIRECTIONS

1. Study the Rating Scale for Confrontation Skill.

2. Rate the responses for Situations One, Two, and Three.

3. Be prepared to discuss your ratings.

RATING SCALE FOR CONFRONTATION SKILL

The terms High (H), Medium (M), and Low (L) will be used to identify the quality of the confrontation responses. The following statements are definitions of High, Medium, and Low conditions of confrontation.

High Conditions of Effective Confrontation (H): The helper indicates differences clearly and points out the discrepancies in one of the following three areas:

1. difference between what helpee says and does,

2. difference between what others say and what helpee does, and

3. difference between helpee's feelings and actual behavior or difference between what helpee says and how helpee feels or looks.

Medium Conditions of Effective Confrontation (M): Hints at the difference but is not clear.

Low Conditions of Effective Confrontation (L): Avoids the differences completely in the conversation.

Situation One

Teenager to Parent: "I've lived here all my life but don't know anybody. Even here at school I just can't seem to make friends. I try to be nice to other kids, but I feel all uncomfortable inside and things just don't go right. Then I tell myself I don't care, people aren't any good, everyone's out for himself. I don't want any friends. Sometimes I think I really mean it."

Helper Responses for Situation One

Rating

_____ 1. "You're in a real bind. You want to make friends but you find you excuse yourself when you don't succeed as you'd like to."

_____ 2. "There's nothing wrong with that. Many people learn to live secluded lives."

_____ 3. "You're concerned because you haven't been able to make friends."

_____ 4. "You're excusing yourself when you find it's difficult to go out to others. You know that you need and want others in your life. As long as you make excuses, you will feel this emptiness."

_____ 5. "Can you tell me what are some of the things you've done to make friends?"

_____ 6. "You can join this club I belong to. We have a small group and need members. You'll make lots of friends and have lots of fun."

_____ 7. "When you tell yourself you don't care, that people aren't any good, you wind up feeling crummy inside."

Write concerns or questions you have as a result of rating responses to Situation One.

_____

_____

Situation Two

Student to Teacher: "I can't see why you gave me a 'C' on my paper. I worked on it for six weeks. I know Joe worked hard on his, too, and you gave him and 'A'. That doesn't seem fair to me."

Helper Responses for Situation Two

Rating

_____ 8. "You don't think 'C' is a fair grade on the paper."

_____ 9. "You've put a lot of effort into this paper and it really upsets you that Joe got the higher grade. Let's look over the objectives I set up and see if your 'C' fits them."

_____ 10. "You feel I wasn't fair in grading your paper."

_____ 11. "You are angry I gave you a 'C' and you think you did as well as Joe, but yet you feel Joe worked very hard also."

Write concerns or questions you have as a result of rating responses to Situation Two.

_____

_____

Situation Three

Hospitalized Patient to Nurse: "I don't know why I am here. I just feel depressed at times and think about hurting myself or others. This is pretty normal for the people I know."

Helper Response for Situation Three

Rating

_____ 12. "You don't think you should be here."

_____ 13. "You have all these feelings but that is pretty normal."

_____ 14. "You don't feel that you should be here yet your family feels scared when you get down and talk about suicide or hurting others."

Write concerns or questions you have as a result of rating responses to Situation Three.

_____

_____

HOMEWORK

Study Exercise 11.3 and be prepared to do it in the next group meeting.

Exercise 11.3

ROLE-PLAYING FOR CONFRONTATION SKILL AND RATING THE HELPER

In this exercise you are going to learn to deal with the skill of confrontation as a helper, helpee, and rater. You will be given different situations to role-play. In one situation you will role-play the helper and illustrate your skill in effective confrontation in that situation. In another situation you will have an opportunity to rate a helper's ability at utilizing effective confronting. In a third situation you will take the role of the helpee who is demonstrating a differing behavior.

GOALS

In this exercise you will learn

1. confrontation skill through role-playing and rating others who are using confrontation skill,

2. to discriminate better among high, medium, and low conditions of effective confrontation, and

3. to utilize different peer helping skills including confrontation skill in a helping relationship.

DIRECTIONS

1. Form clusters of three with one person initially being in the helpee role, another in the helper role, and the third in the rater role.

2. Choose one of the Role-playing Situations found on the next page to role-play in your cluster.

3. Role-play the situation chosen with the helpee describing the situation to the helper and the helper responding by using peer helping skills.

4. Continue the experience through three or four interchanges with the helper sending at least one confrontation message during the dialogue. The rater is to rate only the confrontation message sent by the helper in this exercise. Use Flow Sheet for Rating Confrontation as instructed in Directions 1 through 6.

5. After four or five interchanges, stop the role-playing and have the rater give feedback to the helper as the quality of the confrontation response.

6. Repeat the experience until all members of the training cluster have had an opportunity to play each role. You have a choice as to what situations you wish to use. You may use the same one over again, choose another one from the list of Role-Playing Situations or create one of your own.

7. After you have done this exercise several times and are becoming competent in giving effective confrontation messages, follow your trainer's directions to do an extended role-playing exercise.

8. In the extended dialogue (role-playing) exercise, do the following:

   a. Extend a dialogue over a minimum of eight helper responses.

   b. Use as many of the six peer helping skills as the role-playing situation will permit.

   c. Use a real situation if one of the three cluster members wants help regarding something of concern to him/her.

9. As rater for the extended exercise, use the Flow Sheet for Rating Confrontation and Other Communication Skills found on a separate page later in this exercise (11.3). Follow the directions given there.

ROLE-PLAYING SITUATIONS

Below are listed seven role situations that lend themselves easily to possible confrontation conditions. Before you start working within your cluster of three trainees, choose one or more of the roles and experience how the role develops. Use a helper and helpee as the developers of the role. The rater will rate the effectiveness of the helpers' confrontation behaviors using the Rating Scale for Confrontation Skill provided in Exercise 11.2.

In assuming these roles use extra caution to be certain that the role behavior is not the usual role of the person being portrayed. To do otherwise will result in no discrepancy in the two behaviors and thus no opportunity will exist for confrontation to take place.

1. Role-play a person who often criticizes the behavior of other individuals.

2. Role-play a person who is extremely shy in groups.

3. Role-play a person who frequently embarrasses others by rude remarks and bad table manners.

4. Role-play a person who jokes about the problems of others.

5. Role-play a person who constantly express a great deal of affection for everyone.

6. Role-play a person who is so "nice" that it is "unreal."

7. Role-play a person who is constantly high on pot.

Name _____

Date _____ Hour _____

FLOW SHEET FOR RATING CONFRONTATION

Follow the instructions in Directions 1 through 6. During the role-playing use one of the situations listed in this exercise in section entitled "Role-Playing Situations."

First Role-Play Where You Are Rater

Rating for (Name the Helper) _____

Confrontation Rating (check one) ___H ___M ___L

Reason for Rating: _____

_____

Second Role-Play Where You Are Rater

Rating for (Name the Helper) _____

Confrontation Rating (Check one) ___H ___M ___L

Reason for Rating: _____

_____

Exercise 11.3 (Continued)

Flow Sheet for Rating Confrontation and Other Communication Skills

This flow sheet is to be used for extended dialogue exercises in rating each of the skills you have learned, however place emphasis on the skill of confrontation. Since in any interchange all of the skills must be available when needed, this rating flow sheet enables the rater to rate all of the helper's responses and will help you to understand how confrontation fits into the total helping relationship.

Name ——————

Date —————— Hour ——————

Rating for (name person) ——————

Attending Response			Empathy				Summarizing			Open-Ended			Genuineness ("I" message)			Assertiveness			Confrontation		
H	M	L	Feeling Word	H	M	L	H	M	L	H	M	L	H	M	L	H	M	L	H	M	L
1.																					
2.																					
3.																					
4.																					
5.																					
6.																					
7.																					

Rating for (name person) ——————

1.																					
2.																					
3.																					
4.																					
5.																					
6.																					

HOMEWORK

Study the introduction to Module XII and study exercise 12.1 before the next group meeting.

MODULE XII

Problem Solving

The Eighth Skill in Peer Helping

8 Problem Solving
7 Confrontation
6 Assertiveness
5 Genuineness
4 Questioning
3 Summarizing
2 Empathizing
1 Attending

PROBLEM SOLVING SKILL

As a peer helper, you easily can, at this point, listen to problems and concerns of others. Helping others to explore and understand is a good start in peer helping and often is all that is necessary, because a sounding board may be all your peers need. However, many times listening and understanding does not go far enough. A helpee may need to take some action in order to grow. This action behavior can take the form of problem solving.

If we listen to someone long enough, problem solving becomes an important skill to assist people. Often just to listen is not enough; sometimes people need help in making decisions. Problem solving is the action that brings about change. Without learning the action stage of helping, earlier skills of empathy and attending are sometimes of little value. This module on problem solving will assist you not only in learning the complete problems, but also in learning techniques of "brainstorming", the effect of values on decisions, picking the best solution, and putting the solution into action.

Many ways are available to solve problems and using the communication skills you have learned up to now is one of those ways. When listening is not enough, you will need some other problem-solving techniques. The skill in Module XII will give you new ways in which you can help others arrive at problem-solving action. Notice we didn't say solve their problems for them; rather, the meaning is to help them take the action.

Problem-solving techniques you will be learning enable you to brainstorm, choose the best solution, consider values, and develop a plan of action. You may not want to use all of these techniques each time, but they come in handy when you have done a good job of exploring and understanding and need to take the next step toward behavior change. In addition, learning the problem-solving skill will benefit you as well as your helpee when you want to change your behavior and need ways to make this change.

If the audio tape on problem solving that is a companion to this module is available, you may want to listen to it so that you can use the technique in your everyday problem-solving activity.

Use: This activity can be useful with high school age individuals and adults and can be used as a separate activity for problem-solving unit.

Exercise 12.1

Name _____

Date _____ Hour _____

PROBLEM-SOLVING PROCEDURES

Basic communication skills will be used in problem-solving behaviors. For example, in exploring the problem the helper will use the skills of empathy, attending, and questioning. During the understanding part of problem solving, the helper would use genuineness, summarizing, and confrontation.

GOALS

In this exercise you will learn the seven steps in problem solving.

DIRECTIONS

1. Review the following "Seven Steps in Problem Solving."

2. Note differences in what is being done by the helpee and the helper.

3. Be prepared to discuss the seven steps at the next training session.

SEVEN STEPS IN PROBLEM SOLVING

HELPEE STEPS IN PROBLEM SOLVING	HELPER PROCEDURES AND SKILLS IN PROBLEM SOLVING
Step 1. Explore the Problem	
The helpee explains the initially stated problem, in very general terms.	The helper will use the skills of empathy, attending, and open-ended questioning.
Step 2. Understand the Problem	
The helpee looks at all aspects of the problem, reasons for concerns, and underlying feelings about the different aspects of the problem.	The helper will use the skills of attending, empathy, open-ended questioning, genuineness, and confrontation.

Step 3. Define the Problem

The helpee clearly states the concerns in specific terms as they relate directly to the helpee. The definition needs to refer not only to the dimensions of the problem but to the helpee goals to be achieved by problem solving.

The helper gains agreement about the real concerns through the use of summarizing skill.

Step 4. Brainstorm All Alternatives

The helpee thinks of all possible alternatives without evaluating them. The helpee's goal is to arrive at as many alternatives imaginable.

The helper with the helpee brainstorms all courses of action (alternatives) which can be directed toward solving the defined problem. The helper suggests possible alternatives if helpee is having difficulty and asks open-ended questions to move the helpee into thinking of alternatives.

Step 5. Evaluate Alternatives

The helpee examines the values held. (A value is something that is very important to the helpee. Values help establish priorities and direct you in your choices.) The helpee also examines strengths and weaknesses that relate to each of the alternatives identified in the brainstorming activity.

The helper lists the values that relate to the problem and underlines the most important values of the helpee. The helper lists helpee's strengths as they relate to each alternative. The helper lists helpee's weaknesses in implementing alternatives. The skills of empathy, open-ended questioning, and summarizing are used.

Step 6. Decide on the Best Alternative

The helpee decides the best alternative in light of values that influenced the selection of the alternative. The helpee examines the strength that will

The helper will write the best solution and list the value(s) that are involved in making the decision. The helper lists the

implement the alternative. The helpee answers the following questions about the selected alternatives:

a. Do I have all the data available?

b. Is the alternative specific?

c. Is the alternative believable to me?

d. Does the alternative coincide with my values?

e. Does the alternative help me grow as a person?

f. Is the alternative something I can control?

g. Is the alternative what I want to do?

strength(s) needed to implement the alternative. The helper will ask the helpee the following questions:

a. Do you have all the available data?

b. Is the alternative specific enough?

c. Is the alternative believable and conceivable for you?

d. Does the alternative coincide with your values?

e. Does the alternative help you grow as a person?

f. Is the alternative something you can control?

g. Is the alternative something you want to do?

The helper may use the skills of open-ended questioning and empathy.

Step 7. Implement the Selected Alternative

The helpee will develop a plan of action to implement the best alternative. The helpee will answer the following questions:

a. What are my goals which need to be met in order to solve this problem?

b. What is the first action necessary to put plan into operation?

c. What are the next activities in the plan and what sequence must take place to reach my goal?

The helper will assist the helpee to implement a reasonable plan of action. Please list the answers to the following questions:

a. What goals do you have that are met by this alternative?

b. What is the first action necessary to put the plan into operation?

c. What are the next activities in the plan and in what sequence can you put them to reach your goal?

d. What obstacles are in the way to reaching the goal?

d. What obstacles are in the way to reaching your goals?

e. What strengths do I possess to overcome the obstacles in my way?

e. What strengths do you possess to overcome those obstacles?

f. Who else will be needed to implement the alternative chosen?

f. Who else will be needed to implement the alternative chosen?

g. What time lines are needed to reach my goals?

g. What time lines are needed to put into action?

h. Where are the activities to take place?

h. Where is this alternative to be put into action?

i. When do I take my first action?

i. When are you going to take the first action?

STEP	SKILL(S) USED
1. Exploring the Problem	empathy, attending, open-ended questioning
2. Understanding the Problem	empathy, attending, open-ended questioning, genuineness, confrontation
3. Defining the Problem	summarizing
4. Brainstrorming All Alternatives	open-ended questioning
5. Evaluating Alternatives	open-ended questioning, summarizing
6. Deciding the Best Alternative	empathy, attending, open-ended questioning, summarizing
7. Implementing the Selected Alternative	open-ended questioning, summarizing

HOMEWORK

Study Exercise 12.2 and be prepared to discuss it at the next group meeting.

Exercise 12.2

PROBLEM-SOLVING DIALOGUE

GOAL

In this exercise you will learn to become familiar with the dialogue when using the seven steps in problem solving.

DIRECTIONS

1. Read the example of problem-solving dialogue included in Exercise 12.2.

2. Study how the helper achieves each of the seven steps within the dialogue.

3. Note the ease with which the helper moves from one step into the next.

4. Review the seven steps so as to become familiar with the sequence and a means for achieving each.

EXAMPLE: PROBLEM-SOLVING DIALOGUE

Step 1—Explore the Problem

Helpee: "I don't know what job to get once I get out of school."

Helper: "You're unsure of the kind of job you want?"

Helpee: "Yes, I think I want to get into the medical area but I am not sure."

Helper: "Medical careers turn you on, but you are not sure."

Helpee: "That is what I think I am working toward because I have taken nothing but science courses since I have been in high school."

Helper: "What jobs in the medical field have you considered?"

Helpee: "I have thought about being a doctor but I don't think I could make it, so I guess I will be a nurse."

Step 2—Understand the Problem

Helper: "You really would like to be a doctor, but it might be to much to make it."

Helpee: "Yes. It takes so long to go to school, I don't know whether I have the stamina to make it."

Helper: "You feel uncertain if you have the energy to make it through medical school."

Helpee: "Being a doctor is something I have always wanted to do and my family has been planning on me going."

Helper: "I hear you saying two things—You really want to do it, and you have the support, but you seem to not have the confidence in yourself that you can make it."

Helpee: "Yes, self confidence is something I hardly ever have, I convince myself that I can't do certain things, and it really hurts when I go ahead and try."

Helper: "You put yourself down a lot. I guess I feel uncomfortable when you put yourself down and it causes me to maybe suggest other careers for you that you will have the confidence to do. This concerns me that you may regret it later."

Helpee: "It seems like the more I talk about my lack of confidence, others feel sorry for me and try to tell me I can do it. I don't need a pep talk from others."

Step 3—Define the Problem

Helper: "You feel really confused about your future job, but even more important now is lack of confidence in yourself."

Helpee: "Yes, I guess what I really need to look at is understanding myself and feeling good about how I am so I know myself and can really do something or not do something."

Helper: "Let me check this out—You want to understand your abilities, you want to feel good about yourself now, then you will really be able to work toward a definite career goal."

Helpee: "Yes, that is really where I am now."

Step 4—Brainstorm Alternatives

Helper: "Let's look at some ways to find the answers about yourself and feel good about you. I will write the ideas down and keep notes. Let's not evaluate any of the ideas. Let's just keep notes."

Helpee: "Well, I could sign up for counseling or take some of those courses on understanding yourself." (Helper writes two ideas—"counseling" and "self help course.")

Helper: "You could take a series of tests to see your strengths and weaknesses as far as ability." (Helper writes "testing.")

Helpee: "I could ask my friends what they think about me or I could just spend time thinking about it." (Helper writes "ask friends.")

Helper: "You could ask your family or teachers how they see your abilities." (Helper writes "ask family or teachers.")

Helpee: "I could sign up for one of the Human Potential Groups at School." (Helper writes "Human Potential Groups.")

Step 5—Evaluate Alternatives

Helper: "Let's look at the list of suggested alternatives and then figure if any of your values are applicable to it, then let's look at your strengths and weaknesses that are applicable for each alternative. We can do it by making two charts that will compare each of the qualities with which we are working."

Through working with the helpee, the helper and the helpee have identified important values held by the helpee. In the case illustrated but not included in the Sample Problem-Solving Dialogue, five important values were identified—having independence, gaining an education, doing well on tests, having a family life, and having friends. These five values were used in a chart to examine whether or not each alternative would be appropriate for each value held. The "Comparison Chart of Values for Each Alternative" is shown for the Sample Problem-Solving Dialogue.

COMPARISON CHART OF VALUES FOR EACH ALTERNATIVE

Alternatives (as identified in Step 4)	Value 1 Independence	Value 2 Education	Value 3 Do well on tests	Value 4 Family Life	Value 5 Friends	Total Yes Responses
1. Counseling	Yes	Yes	No	No	Yes	3
2. Self-help Course	Yes	Yes	Yes	No	Yes	4
3. Testing	No	Yes	Yes	No	No	2
4. Ask Family	No	No	No	Yes	No	1
5. Ask Friends	No	No	No	No	Yes	1
6. Human Potential Group	Yes	Yes	Yes	No	No	3

Following the completion of the "Comparison Chart of Values for Each Alternative," the helper used another chart to enable the helpee to examine strengths and weaknesses of the helpee as related to each alternative. The "Comparison Chart of Alternatives to Strengths and Weaknesses" is shown for the Sample Problem-Solving Dialogue but the dialogue which occurred during development of the chart is not shown.

COMPARISON CHART OF ALTERNATIVES TO STRENGTHS AND WEAKNESSES

Alternatives (as identified in Step 4)	Strengths (applicable to each alternative)	Weaknesses (applicable to each alternative)	Strongest Potential Character
1. Counseling	Solve things myself	Time (lack of)	Strength
2. Self-help Course	Learn quickly	Time (lack of)	Weakness
3. Testing	Do well on tests	Fear of results	Strength
4. Ask Family	Communicate openly	Can't trust	Weaknesses
5. Ask Friends	Leadership	Can't trust	Weakness
6. Human Potential Group	Like to talk	Time (lack of)	Weakness

Step 6—Decide on the Best Alternative

Helper: "Underline the top value and best strength. There are several choices but it looks like your best choice might be the Human Potential Group and a self-help course."

Helpee: "Yes, because I enjoy learning about myself and learning in general. I am not afraid to talk about myself and learn quickly."

Helper: "Let me ask you some questions about your decision. Is the alternative specific? Is it clear?"

Helpee: "Yes."

Helper: "Is it something that is believable? Could you do it?"

Helpee: "Yes."

Helper: "Does this alternative coincide with your values?"

Helpee: "Yes."

Helper: "Will the alternative help you grow as a person?"

Helpee: "Yes."

Helper: "Is it something that is in the realm of your control."

Helpee: "Yes."

Helper: "Do you want to do it?"

Helpee: "Yes."

Step 7—Implement the Selected Alternative

Helper: "Now comes the hardest part of figuring out ways of implementing alternatives. Will the alternative help you meet your goals of understanding yourself now and feeling good about yourself?"

Helpee: "Yes."

Helper: "What steps must you take to accomplish it?"

Helpee: "I can sign up for Human Potential Group with my counselor and probably go see the counselor about a self-help course."

Helper: "I wonder what strengths you possess that will help you overcome your lack of confidence."

Helpee: "Well I like to learn and I stick to things once I have decided."

Helper: "Will anyone else be involved?"

Helpee: "My counselor."

Helper: "When are you going to see the counselor?"

Helpee: "This week because the Human Potential Group starts soon and I hope to take the course in the summer."

Helper: "Where do you go?"

Helpee: "Guidance Center."

Helper: "What is your first step?"

Helpee: "Talk to the counselor."

HOMEWORK

1. Study the sample dialogue again if any of the seven steps is not understood.

2. Review purposes for each of the seven steps and the means for achieving each.

3. Study Exercise 12.3 and come to next group meeting prepared to discuss and to follow through on direction provided.

Exercise 12.3

Name _____

Date _____ Hour _____

ROLE-PLAYING PRACTICE
FOR
PROBLEM-SOLVING SKILL

GOALS

In this exercise you as a helper will

1. practice the seven steps in problem solving.

2. assist a helpee in using the seven steps in problem solving in a real situation.

3. assist the helpee in identifying the appropriate information for each step as it occurs.

4. learn to record appropriate information for each step as it occurs.

DIRECTIONS

1. When instructed to do so by the trainer, divide into clusters of two; one person will be the helper and the other the helpee.

2. Have the helpee select a real situation which will require problem solving so as to enter into a dialogue with the helper.

3. Begin the problem-solving dialogue between the helpee and helper using the seven steps identified in this Module 12.

4. Record as the dialogue proceeds. The helper will write in the space provided the appropriate information for each step as it occurs. (Specific directions are provided on the Flow Sheets for each step.)

5. Reverse roles and repeat the role-playing experience after having gone all the way through the seven steps. The trainer may ask for discussion among all trainees before the second roleplaying practice.

6. Be prepared to discuss the experience within the total group each time after having gone through the seven steps.

FLOW SHEETS

The Flow Sheets for use during the role-playing are on the pages which follow. Directions and an example are provided for each of the seven steps in Problem-Solving Skill. The helper is to record information on the Flow Sheets as the dialogue progresses.

Step 1. Explore the Problem

DIRECTIONS

During the problem-solving dialogue, record the problem(s) as stated by the helpee. The recording is to be done by the helper.

EXAMPLES

(Taken from the Example Problem-Solving Dialogue, Step 1 in Exercise 12.2.)

1. Undecided career

2. Wants medical field but unsure of which job

NOTES FROM ROLE-PLAYING (Notes are to be taken by the helper.)

_____

_____

_____

_____

_____

_____

_____

_____

Name _____

Date _____ Hour _____

Step 2. Understand the Problem

DIRECTIONS

Take notes on various aspects and feelings of the problem as identified by the helpee.

EXAMPLES

(Taken from the Example Problem-solving Dialogue, Step 2 in Exercise 12.2.)

1. Takes too long to become a doctor

2. Lacks stamina (energy)

3. Family support

4. Have desire

5. Lacks self-confidence

6. Puts self down

7. Friends show concern

NOTES FROM ROLE-PLAYING (Notes are to be taken by the helper.)

_____

_____

_____

_____

_____

_____

Step 3. Define the Problem

DIRECTIONS

Write the problem and goals in specific terms as identified in the dialogue between the helpee and helper.

EXAMPLES

(Taken from the Example Problem-solving Dialogue, Step 3 in Exercise 12.2.)

Problem--confidence in self

Goals: to understand own abilities

        to feel good about self

        to work toward a definite career goal

NOTES FROM ROLE-PLAYING (Notes are to be taken by the helper.)

_____

_____

_____

_____

_____

_____

_____

_____

_____

Step 4. Brainstorm Alternatives

DIRECTIONS

1. Record all possible alternatives identified by the helpee and helper during the dialogue.

2. Do not evaluate any alternative during the Brainstorming, Step 4.

EXAMPLES

(Taken from the Example Problem-solving Dialogue, Step 4 in Exercise 12.2.)

1. Counseling

2. Self-help course

3. Testing

4. Ask friends

5. Ask family or teachers

6. Human Potential Groups

NOTES FROM ROLE-PLAYING (Notes are to be taken by helper.)

_____

_____

_____

_____

_____

_____

Step 5. Evaluate Alternatives

DIRECTIONS

1. Use the "Comparison Chart of Values for Each Alternative" to assist the helper.

2. Complete the chart (helper does the writing) with the assistance of the helpee from information supplied during the dialogue, i.e., values held by the helpee and whether or not (yes or no) each value is applicable to each alternative identified in Step 4, Brainstorm Alternatives.

3. After the helpee's major values are identified <u>underline</u> the value which the helpee says is the most important.

4. Review the chart with the helpee so that the helpee can evaluate alternatives.

EXAMPLE

A completed "Comparison Chart of Values for Each Alternative" is provided in Exercise 12.2 for the example Problem-solving Dialogue.

COMPARISON CHART OF VALUES FOR EACH ALTERNATIVE
(Helper completes during role-playing practice.)

Alternatives (as identified in Step 4)	Value 1*	Value 2*	Value 3*	Value 4*	Value 5*	Total Yes Responses
1.						
2.						
3.						
4.						
5.						
6.						

*The one to five major values held by the helpee will need to be written in as column headings (e.g., Value 1, Independence is desired).

Name _____

Date _____ Hour _____

DIRECTIONS

1. Use the "Comparison Chart of Alternatives to Strengths and Weaknesses" to assist the helpee.

2. With the assistance of the helpee complete the chart using the information supplied during the dialogue, i.e., the helpee's greatest strength and greatest weakness associated with each alternative. Then identify which of the two (strength or weakness) is the strongest potential characteristic.

3. After the chart is complete, underline the strength which the helpee says is the most appropriate for this situation.

4. Review the chart with the helpee so that the helpee can evaluate alternatives.

EXAMPLE

A completed "Comparison Chart of Alternatives and Strengths and Weaknesses" is provided in Exercise 12.2 for the example Problem-solving Dialogue.

COMPARISON CHART OF ALTERNATIVES TO STRENGTHS AND WEAKNESSES
(Helper completes the chart during role-playing practice.)

Alternatives (as identified in Step 4)	Strengths (applicable to each alternative	Weaknesses (applicable to each alternative	Strongest Potential Character

Step 6. Decide on the Best Alternative

DIRECTIONS

1. Have and/or assist the helpee in choosing one or two alternatives from Step 5 that fit the helpee's values and strengths.

2. Circle on the charts completed in Step 5 the one or two alternatives chosen.

3. Proceed with the dialogue to achieve Step 6 in Problem Solving.

4. Record the helpee's answers to the important questions raised in Step 6.

5. If the questions raised cannot be answered and answered in the affirmative (yes), then return to the appropriate step where the question(s) can be clarified.

INFORMATION AND QUESTIONS (Helper records as the helpee explores the questions.)

1. What values led me (the helpee) to the decision?

_____

_____

2. What are my (the helpee's) strength(s) to assist in implementing the alternative(s)?

_____

_____

3. Please check the appropriate answer to the following:

   Yes   No   ?

   _____ _____ _____   a.   Do I (the helpee) have all the data?

   _____ _____ _____   b.   Is the alternative specific?

   _____ _____ _____   c.   Is the alternative believable to me (the helpee)?

   _____ _____ _____   d.   Does the alternative coincide with my (the helpee's) values?

   _____ _____ _____   e.   Does the alternative help me (the helpee) grow as a person?

   _____ _____ _____   f.   Is the alternative something I (the helpee) can control?

   _____ _____ _____   g.   Is the alternative what I (the helpee) want to do?

Step 7. Implement the Selected Alternative

DIRECTIONS

1. As helper, assist the helpee in examining what is necessary and how to proceed in implementing the alternative(s).

2. Record the information as the helpee identifies each of the essential items to consider in Step 7.

3. After the information is recorded on this page, review the information with the helpee.

NOTES FROM ROLE-PLAYING (Notes are to be taken by helper.)

1. Goal(s) to be met: _____

_____

_____

2. Procedure—activity by activity in sequential order:

First action: _____

_____

_____

Additional activities (list in sequential order): _____

_____

_____

3. Obstacles in my way: _____

_____

_____

4. My strengths to overcome obstacles: _____

_____

_____

5. Person or persons needed to help implement plan: _____

_____

_____

6. Activities to perform: _____

_____

_____

7. Estimated time lines: _____

_____

_____

8. Date and time for my first action: _____

_____

_____

HOMEWORK

1. Study Exercise 12.4 and complete the seven steps as requested.

2. Be prepared to discuss your material.

3. Obtain your group leader's approval before implementation of your proposed steps.

Exercise 12.4

Name _____

Date _____ Hour _____

PLAN OF ACTION
TO ASSIST HELPEE IN PROBLEM SOLVING

GOALS

In this exercise you will learn

1. to develop a plan of action for assisting another person in problem solving.

2. to develop a sequence of activities which are meaningful and in developmental order.

DIRECTIONS

1. Identify a person whom you will assist.

2. Identify in general terms the person's problem(s) with which you believe you can assist the person. List these under Step 1 in the space provided.

3. Develop a plan of action for assisting the person in the problem solving. List the plan under Step 2 in the space provided.

4. Write the plan of action in the space provided under Steps 3 through 7.

5. Have the plan of action approved by your trainer before you follow the seven steps in problem solving, that is, before you do peer helping with the person.

STEPS IN THE PLAN OF ACTION

Step 1. Explore the Problem.

List in general, the helpee's problem(s) as you know the problem(s), and list only the ones with which you believe you can assist.

_____

_____

_____

Step 2. Understand the Problem(s)

List in general, plans you have to assist the helpee in fully understanding the problem(s).

_____

_____

_____

Step 3. Define the Problem

Assuming your general outline of problem(s) is correct, write the problem(s) in specific terms similar to the wording you will expect the helpee to use.

_____

_____

_____

Step 4. Brainstorm Alternatives

If your statement(s) of Problem(s) is/are correct, what brainstorming alternatives do you have for possible actions for solving the problem? Do not evaluate the feasibility of the alternatives. List the alternatives.

_____

_____

_____

Step 5. Evaluate Alternatives

Outline your procedures for having the helpee evaluate the alternatives which will be identified during the brainstorming dialogue.

_____

_____

_____

Step 6. Decide on the Best Alternative

Outline your procedures for having the helpee decide which one or two alternatives will be seriously considered for implementation.

_____

_____

_____

Step 7. Implement the Selected Alternative

Outline your procedures for assisting the helpee in developing sequential actions for implementing the alternative chosen.

_____

_____

_____

Identify the people whom you believe may need to be involved if the helpee's problem is developed to a satisfactory problemsolving solution.

_____

_____

_____

HOMEWORK

1. After obtaining approval for your plan of action, implement your plan during the week.

2. Come prepared to report progress at the next group meeting.

3. Study the introduction to Module XIII and complete Strategy Development 1 before the next group meeting.

Date _____   Teacher's Approval of Plan _____

Unit **C**

*IMPLEMENTING
A
PROGRAM*

IMPLEMENTING A PROGRAM

Now that you have developed helping skills, you are probably anxious to put them into action. The first Strategy assists you in setting framework to put all of your skills to good use. It will help you organize your program and help you become clear of your role(s) in helping others. Keep in mind as you begin to help others, you must take care of yourself so to reduce "burnout."

Your trainer will help you develop some ethical guidelines for you to follow as you begin to set up a feedback system for your trainer.

One skill that can be put to use now is the skill of conflict mediation. As you work with individuals and groups, one theme that is prevalent in our society is conflict. This Strategy Development 2 will help you learn how to solve conflicts in your own life and also help you set up a formal program within your peer helping program. You might find yourself working with family and friends as you help them solve conflicts.

> *"Progress can only happen if you take risks. You can't get to second base with your foot on first base."*
>
> *Baxter*

MODULE XIII

Strategy Development

STRATEGY DEVELOPMENT
SD 1

PUTTING PEER HELPING
INTO ACTION

Now that you have learned the skills of attending, empathy, summarizing, questioning, genuineness, assertiveness, confrontation, and problem solving, you will want to put these skills into action. Uses of these skills are limitless. They can be useful to you not only in peer helping but also with your family, friends, or co-workers. These skills are just the beginning of your learning skills being a helper.

As a peer helper you may be assigned helper tasks by your trainer, or you may choose to establish you own helping relationships. We hope both will occur, thus making maximum use of skills you have learned.

You need to be involved in designing your peer helping activities. The "Organizing Peer Helping Flow Sheet" is designed to help you set your own goals in peer helping for the week. Work with your supervisor to set these goals, and be flexible to change. You will feel good at the end of each goal-setting period if you look at how much of the goal you actually accomplished and understand how to implement action differently the next time to accomplish even more.

Participating in your own helping tasks and responsibilities is an important part of your training. You are responsible not only for setting up helping opportunities with your trainer's assistance but also for establishing your peer-helping goals and outcomes on a weekly or monthly basis. Only by setting goals and following through to their completion will you continue to improve your newly learned skills. Goal setting, acting on those goals, and checking on your success in meeting them are helpful ways to bring about your success as a peer helper. You will have a record of what you wish to accomplish and how well you have succeeded as well as an account of your growth and accomplishments. By setting goals and checking on your progress toward reaching them, you will identify those areas in which you need additional help or skill building.

Before proceeding to implementation you will need to check your skills. At the start of your peer helping training you took a pretest; now you can take the posttest. If you can answer the items easily and if you do well on the posttest, you will be able to use your newly acquired skills immediately. If you have difficulty in answering these questions or if you do not do well on the posttest, perhaps you could join another group of trainees and repeat the program. Trainers can help you decide on a plan of action; talk with yours.

> *"Progress always involves risk; you can't steal second base and keep your foot on first."*
> Frederick Wilcox

Use: This module is to be used after trainees have completed the previous twelve modules.

Name _____

Date _____ Hour _____

POSTTEST COMMUNICATIONS EXERCISE

A HELPFUL PERSON IS—a person getting along with himself/herself and one who is genuine (not phony) when talking with others. When he/she talks with other people, he/she is understanding of and respects the feelings of others. This person seems very confident and his/her actions are natural. He/she can adjust to many different kinds of people, but is still capable of letting one know his/her feelings at the right time.

DIRECTIONS

1. Rate responses on the following pages. Material includes ten statements which you are to assume are made to you by other persons.

2. For Statements 1 through 5, rate each of the four given responses to the statement in order of the statement's helpfulness.
   A rating of Low (L) means no help;
   Medium (M) means some help;
   High (H) means a high degree of help.

   Low (L) response: The response is not helpful to another person.

   Medium (M) response: The response is of little help to another person.

   High (H) response: The response is extremely helpful—meets all the conditions described for a helpful statement.

POSTTEST FOR ADOLESCENTS
(For Adult use, see Statements 1B through 10B.)

Statement 1A

"My parents won't let me go over there at night. They say I'll get into trouble if I hang around with those kids."

Responses for Statement 1A

__ 1a.   What have you done that makes your parents not trust you?

__ 1b.   What they don't know won't hurt them. Your mistake is telling them too much about what you do.

_ 1c. It's hard sometimes to accept your parents' ideas on things.

_ 1d. It is upsetting because your parents won't let you be with the kids. It's like they don't trust your judgment.

Statement 2A

"Those snobs won't ask me. . .they think they are better than me. . .who needs 'em anyhow!"

Responses for Statement 2A

_ 2a. Why don't you stop pouting about it and find somebody else?

_ 2b. It makes you mad to think that others think you're not good enough to be with them.

_ 2c. You'd like to be involved with them but they show no interest, it makes you wonder about really what to do.

_ 2d. That's the approach I take with stuck up people. . .just get as far away as I can.

Statement 3A

"My grades are horrible. My parents have grounded me for a month, and I've lost my allowance. I don't know what else could go wrong."

Response for Statement 3A

_ 3a. This predicament has you feeling so low it makes you wonder if anything else could go wrong.

_ 3b. Don't worry, there's always something worse to come along.

_ 3c. I know what you mean. I've had that same thing happen to me. You feel just like everything is sour at once.

_ 3d. Quit feeling sorry for yourself. It won't help much.

Statement 4A

"I try so hard to be good in P.E. but I get so embarrassed because I don't play football."

Responses for Statement 4A

__ 4a. sometimes you just have to face the idea that you can't be good in football.

__ 4b. Sometimes it's hard to feel like you're good in football even though you do your best.

__ 4c. Why don't you try to get out of P.E.?

__ 4d. What have you done to learn to play football?

Statement 5A

"I have some new friends that my parents don't like because of their long hair, but they really don't know them."

Responses for Statement 5A

__ 5a. What have you done that makes your parents not like your friends?

__ 5b. Why don't you go along with your parents and find new friends?

__ 5c. It makes you feel that your parents don't trust you to choose new friends.

__ 5d. You should go ahead and be friends anyway.

DIRECTIONS FOR STATEMENTS 6A THROUGH 10A

For statements 6A through 10A, write what you consider a helpful response to the person.

Statement 6A

"I should have kept my mouth shut. My friend promised she would not mention it to anyone and now the whole school knows. I would really like to beat her up."

Write what you would say: _____

_____

_____

Statement 7A

"I really hate this school. My other school I went to last year was so great, and now I feel like I don't even want to come to school."

Write what you would say: _____

_____

_____

Statement 8A

"I really don't like to share a room with my brother. He is so messy and inconsiderate of me."

Write what you would say: _____

_____

_____

Statement 9A

"I really hate my first hour teacher. He says I can't pass his class. I sure would like to get out of his class."

Write what you would say: _____

_____

_____

Statement 10A

"I wish Mom would leave me alone and let me do what I want to do. She always has to give me the third degree when I want to go somewhere."

Write what you would say: _____

_____

_____

POSTTEST FOR ADULTS

Statement 1B

"My boss is giving me a hard time, no matter how much I do, he always finds something else that I need to do."

Responses for Statement 1B

__ 1a.   What have you done that always makes your boss find additional things for you to do?

__ 1b.   What your boss thinks is not important. Just tell him to buzz off.

__ 1c.   It's hard at times to accept feedback from your boss.

__ 1d.   It is frustrating that you work so hard, and your boss gives you a hard time.

Statement 2B

"I am new here and I am so lonely. I am afraid to make friends because I always get hurt."

Responses for Statement 2B

__ 2a.   Why don't you just make friends anyway?

__ 2b.   Here you run from people and you don't have friends.

__ 2c.   You feel really lonely because you don't have friends even you are afraid to reach out because you might get hurt.

Statement 3B

"I just lost my job. I had an automobile accident that totaled my car, I don't know what else could go wrong."

Responses to statement 3B

__ 3a.   Quit feeling sorry for yourself. It won't help a lot.

__ 3b.   You are really burned out because you lost your job and your transportation.

__ 3c.   It seems like everything is wrong.

Statement 4B

"I try so hard to lose weight, no matter what I do I can't keep it off.

Responses to Statement 4B

__ 4a. Just quit trying and accept yourself.

__ 4b. You would like to lose weight.

__ 4c. You feel discouraged because no matter what you do to lose weight, you can't keep it off.

Statement 5B

"I don't like the kids that my son is hanging around with. They are always in trouble."

Responses to Statement 5B

__ 5a. Just tell him that he can't hang around them.

__ 5b. What kind of trouble are they in?

__ 5c. You are concerned about the kids your son hangs around with because they are always in trouble.

Statement 6B

"I have a co-worker who can't keep her mouth shut no matter what I tell her she tells everyone."

Write what you would say: _____

_____

_____

Statement 7B

"I really hate my job. It seems like there is nothing more that I like about it anymore. I am just stuck."

Name _____

Date _____ Hour _____

Write what would you say: _____
_____
_____

Statement 8B

"It is a real hassle going to work everyday. There is always pressure to get things done."

Write what would you say: _____
_____
_____

Statement 9B

"My kids are driving me crazy. They are always in trouble. It is hard being a single parent."

Write what would you say: _____
_____
_____

Statement 10B

"I just found out that I am going to have to have an operation. I do not like being in hospitals. I don't like needles either."

Write what would you say: _____
_____
_____

HOMEWORK

1. Complete Exercise SD 1.2 before the next group meeting.

2. Come to the next group meeting prepared to discuss

ORGANIZING FOR PEER HELPING

Now that the training program is completed, you will want to use your newly developed skills. Goal setting is a way to get things done, to change, to become the kind of person you want to be. Each week in our advanced training session we will be setting peer helper goals and sharing our results with other group members. These goals are your goals for you to achieve. The emphasis is upon your making the changes you want so as to become the kind of person you want to be. The process includes the following parts:

1. You select a goal you want to reach.

2. You act—carry out your goal.

3. You experience the satisfaction of completing your goal.

4. This satisfaction encourages you to set another goal.

5. You act—carry out the next goal.

6. So the cycle continues and with each new goal comes a greater sense of satisfaction and achievement.

You can use simple guidelines for setting goals. The guidelines can become criteria for checking your goals easily and quickly. Your criteria for checking should include the following:

1. Conceivable: capable of being put into words.

2. Believable: acceptable as appropriate to your value.

3. Achievable: can be accomplished with your present strengths.

4. Controllable: does not depend upon a specific response from another person in order to achieve it. (The exception is when working on group projects.)

5. Measurable: can be observed.

6. Desirable: something you really want to do.

7. Specifiable and stated with no alternatives: not optional and one at a time.

8. Developmental, growth producing: not injurious to self or others in society.

When your goal includes the criteria listed, you have a better chance of completing the goal successfully. As you set goals, set them so that you will be using your newly developed skills in helping other people. In so doing, you will be helping yourself to become the kind of person you want to be.

EXAMPLES

The following are examples of goals which have been established by trainees. You will need to set your own. Start with some that you can initiate immediately.

1. My goal is to listen better to others and to gain an understanding of what they are truly saying.

2. My goal is to be better able to express the true feelings of others.

3. My goal is to be better able to understand the needs of others.

4. My goal is to become more aware of how and when what I do or say produces a communication stopper with another person.

GOALS

In this exercise you will

1. learn criteria for checking your goals.

2. write goals for yourself to achieve.

3. check yourself on progress in achieving your goals.

4. organize your peer helping activities through establishing your goals.

DIRECTIONS

1. Decide on a goal for yourself. The goal is to include using your peer helping skills.

2. Decide on the time line (beginning and ending dates) for your concentrated efforts to achieve the goal.

3. Check your goal against the criteria for a goal.

4. Discuss your goal and plan for action with your training group.

5. Have your trainer check the goal after you have completed it.

Name _____

Date _____ Hour _____

Goal and Plan for Action

1. My goal is _____

    _____

2. Time line—dates for concentrated effort to achieve goal

    Starting _____   Achieved by _____

3. Criteria for a goal applied to my goal (check each and comment if appropriate.)

		Yes	No	Comment (if appropriate)
a.	Conceivable	____	____	_____
b.	Believable	____	____	_____
c.	Achievable	____	____	_____
d.	Controllable	____	____	_____
e.	Measurable	____	____	_____
f.	Desirable	____	____	_____
g.	Specifiable and stated with no alternative	____	____	_____
h.	Developmental growth producing	____	____	_____

4. Plan for achieving goal (Note: Review items included in Step 7 of "Seven Steps in Problem Solving" in Module XII.)

    a. What is the first action that is necessary in order to put my plan for achieving the goal into operation?

    _____

    _____

b. What are the next activities and in what sequence must these activities take place to reach my goal?

_____

_____

c. What obstacles are in my way to reaching my goal?

_____

_____

d. What strengths do I possess to overcome the obstacles in my way?

_____

_____

e. Who else will be needed to implement my plan? With what person or persons will I work so as to achieve my goal?

_____

_____

f. What are the activities and where are they to take place?

_____

_____

g. When do I take my first action?

_____

_____

5. Trainer's Comments:

Date _____   Approved_____   Suggest Changing_____

(Trainer) Signed _____

HOMEWORK

Implement your plan for helping before your next group meeting and complete the "Self Analysis" in Exercise SD 1.3

Name _____

Date _____ Hour _____

IMPLEMENTING MY PEER HELPER PLAN

GOALS

In this exercise you will

1. implement your plan for helping.

2. obtain feedback from other trainees as to strengths of your implementation.

3. identify means to improve your plan for next time you use it.

DIRECTIONS

1. Before the next group meeting, implement your plan as developed in Exercise SD 1.2.

2. Complete the Self Analysis included in this exercise.

3. Grade yourself on progress toward achieving your goal.

4. Identify significant happenings in your behavior which have and/or have not contributed to your progress.

5. Come to the next group meeting prepared to discuss the implementation of your plan and what happened.

6. Be prepared to share with your group members strengths and means for improving plans.

SELF EVALUATION

1. Grade yourself as to your achievement of your goal.

    _____
    0%   25%   50%   75%   100%

2. What has been the most significant happenings in your behavior which has contributed to the progress you have made?

    _____

    _____

3. How can you in the future emphasize the positiveness that you identified in the previous item?

    _____

    _____

4. What have been obstacles in your achievement of your goal?

    _____

    _____

5. How have you overcome those obstacles, if you have, or what might you do to help overcome the obstacles which remain?

    _____

    _____

HOMEWORK

Review Exercise SD 1.4 and come to the next group meeting prepared to identify a peer helper role for yourself.

Exercise SD 1.4

Name _____

Date _____ Hour _____

WHAT IS YOUR ROLE?

You now have the skills to help others in a variety of ways. To help you apply those skills you will need to consider peer helping roles that you would like to do.

GOAL

In this exercise you will identify roles that you would like to do.

DIRECTIONS

1. Look at the list of possible roles and check the ones that you would like to do.

   Welcome a new student.

   ___ Be a special friend to others.

   ___ Be a mentor to those new on the job.

   ___ Be a volunteer.

   ___ Be a one-on-one helper to those who need help.

   ___ Be a conflict mediator.

   ___ Be a Big Brother/Big Sister.

   ___ Others (Specify)

   _____   .

   _____

2. Work with your trainer to set up goals for the future.

3. Cluster into groups of three and role-play one of the following situations:

a. You have just met a new member of your group (school, business, organization), and you are known in the group as a peer helper to new members. Role-play how you would start in your peer helper role with the new member.

b. You are a mentor to a person. Role-play how you would interact with the person.

c. You have been asked to be a special friend to a younger person. Role-play how you would approach this.

d. You have been asked to volunteer your time to a local homeless shelter. Role-play how you would approach this.

e. You have been asked to be a Big Brother or Big Sister to someone who doesn't have a family. Role-play how you would approach this.

f. Other

4. Change roles and repeat until all trainees have been in a peer helper role.

5. Following the role-playing, share with one another the strengths of the peer helper and possible means of being more helpful if such a role ever did become one for you to fulfill.

HOMEWORK

Work through Exercise SD 1.5 as much as you can before the next group meeting.

Exercise SD 1.5

Name _____

Date _____ Hour _____

TAKING CARE OF YOURSELF

Listening to others is not an easy task. At times, working with others in distress can cause stress in you. While you are listening to others, it is important to set aside your own feelings and concerns and totally focus on them. While you are doing this, you are taking care of the other person, but you are not being taken care of.

One way of taking care of yourself is setting limits to your time for helping others and finding a balance in your life. At times, you may want to say no to others who need you and at times you may need to have some balance. You also need a helper at times and positive support at times.

GOALS

In this exercise you will

1. learn about your own support system.

2. learn how to bring balance into your life.

DIRECTIONS

1. Make a list of things you need from others.

   a. Fun

   b. Honesty

   c. Love

   d. _____

   e. _____

   f. _____

2. Make a list of people you like to have around you.

_____   _____

_____   _____

3. On the chart below, list the people you like for support, the needs each fulfills for you, the one of you who makes the contact, the frequency of support you gain, and the results obtained.

MY SUPPORT SYSTEM

People I like for support	Needs fulfilled	Contact made by	How often	Results obtained

4. Discuss with your training group what you learned about your current support system.

5. What other kind of support do you need for balance?

6. Make a list of people who help you and how they help.

HOMEWORK

1. Decide ways that you can balance your life more effectively, and set some goals to reach that balance in such things as

   a. Work and play

   b. Stress and calm

   c. Taking care of others and taking care of self

2. Study Exercise SD 1.6 and be prepared to discuss it at the next group meeting.

Name _____

Date _____ Hour _____

LOGO AND NAME FOR HELPERS

GOAL

In this exercise you will create a logo for your peer helping group.

DIRECTIONS

1. Brainstorm ideas for the name for your peer helping group. Answer the following questions, and they may help you in the brainstorming.

   a. What is the purpose of your group?

   b. What are some of the characteristics of members of the group?

   c. What are the needs of the people we serve?

   d. What pictures come to mind when you think about your group?

   e. What colors do you like?

2. On chalkboard or newsprint on the wall write the following categories

   Purpose
   Characteristics
   People we serve
   Pictures
   Colors

   a. Work in twos on each area for 5 minutes, writing whatever comes to mind.

   b. Move to the next category for 5 minutes etc., until you have written on all of them.

3. Vote on the name of your group and the symbol for your group

   Examples: PAL—Peer Assisted Leaders
   RAPP—Resolve All Problems Peacefully

4. Work in twos to sketch out a logo.

5. Share all ideas about the logo with the group and vote on the logo.

6. Assign someone to design final draft of logo to be used on announcements T-shirts, notices, brochures, etc.

Name

_____

Logo

HOMEWORK

Study Exercise SD 1.7 and be prepared to discuss it and follow the directions when the group next meets.

Exercise SD 1.7

Name _____

Date _____ Hour _____

ETHICAL GUIDELINES

GOALS

In this exercise you will

1. learn about the National Peer Helpers Association (NPHA) ethical guidelines.

2. participate in establishing our own "Code of Friendship"

DIRECTIONS

1. Review the NPHA "Code of Ethics for Peer Helpers" which is produced on the back of this sheet.

NATIONAL PEER HELPERS ASSOCIATION
CODE OF ETHICS*
FOR PEER HELPERS

Peer Helpers shall be people of personal integrity. As a minimum, the NPHA believes the peer helpers Code of Ethics shall contain the following and be evidenced by a commitment to and pursuit of:

1. A philosophy which upholds peer helping as an effective way to address the needs and conditions of people.

2. The individual's right to dignity, self-development, and self-direction.

3. Supervision and support from professional staff while involved in the program.

4. The development of a nurturing personality which:
    *   Reflects a positive role model and healthy lifestyle (i.e., development and observation
        of a set of norms which guide behavior while in the program).
    *   Rejects the pursuit of personal power, elitist status, or gain at the expense of others.
    *   Strive, to exemplify the peer helping philosophy in all life situations.

5. Maintenance of confidentiality of information imparted during the course of program-related activities. While confidentiality is the norm, certain exceptions shall be referred immediately to the professional staff. These exceptions include the following:

    *   Situations involving real or potential danger to the safety or well-being of the peer helper, helpee, or others.

    *   Child abuse, sexual abuse, and other situations involving legal requirements of disclosure.

    *   Severe family dysfunction, psychotic behavior, extreme drug or alcohol abuse, and any other problems beyond the experience and expertise of the peer helper.

6. Personal Safety

    Peer helpers must recognize, report, and know techniques to deal with potential threats to their emotional or physical well-being.

*A CODE OF ETHICS IS AN AGREEMENT AMONG THOSE WHO COMMIT TO THE PROGRAM AS TO THE NORMS WHICH SHALL GUIDE THEIR BEHAVIOR DURING THEIR INVOLVEMENT IN THE PROGRAM.

2. Divide into groups of two people and examine each of the following situations. Then identify which ethical statement was violated.

SITUATIONS

a. A peer helper was listening to another person tell about a family problem. The peer helper later at a social event went up to the family member who was in conflict with the person with whom they were talking and started discussing the problem.

  —————————————————————————————

  —————————————————————————————

b. The peer helper drinks alcohol excessively on the weekend.

  —————————————————————————————

  —————————————————————————————

c. The peer helper is using his/her position to get special favors from the teachers.

  —————————————————————————————

  —————————————————————————————

d. The peer helper is making fun of someone he/she has been assigned to help.

e. The peer helper has been talking with someone who is thinking about committing suicide and tries to help the person without referring to someone else.

f. The peer helper has been called by someone in trouble to meet the person at a secret place to help him/her.

g. Make up two of your own situations.

  (1) ————————————————————————————

     ————————————————————————————

  (2) ————————————————————————————

     ————————————————————————————

3. Based on the NPHA ethical statement, develop your own ethical guidelines which you may call "Code of Friendship." Space is provided on this sheet.

CODE OF FRIENDSHIP

1. _____

_____

_____

2. _____

_____

_____

3. _____

_____

_____

4. _____

_____

_____

DATE _____   **NAME** _____

HOMEWORK

1. Participate in a peer helper activity.

2. Then complete the Feedback Flow Sheet in Exercise SD 1.8 and submit it to your trainer at the next group meeting.

3. Study the introduction to "Assisting Others Through Conflict Mediation," SD 2.

4. Complete Exercise SD 2.1 before the next group meeting and come prepared to discuss the topic of conflict mediation.

Exercise SD 1.8

Name _____

Date _____ Hour _____

PEER HELPER FEEDBACK FLOW SHEET

GOALS

In this exercise you will

1. learn to record and rate your behaviors during peer helping sessions.

2. become aware of the skills you are using effectively and the ones that you need to improve. This goal can be achieved by reviewing several of your completed "Peer Helping Feedback Flow Sheets."

DIRECTIONS

As you work as a peer helper, complete this flow sheet after each peer helping contact and submit it to your trainer at the next session.

FLOW SHEET FOR PEER HELPER CONTACT*

Date of Peer Helping Contact: _____

Time of Contact (Hour): _____

Meeting Number with this Person (Circle):

                          First   Second   Third   Fourth   Fifth

Location Where Meeting Occurred: _____

General Statement of Person's Problem or Reason for Contact: _____

_____

Skills Used: Please rate your behavior during your peer helping session by checking high, medium, or low for each of the skills.

	High	Medium	Low
1. Attending	_____	_____	_____
2. Empathy	_____	_____	_____
3. Summarizing	_____	_____	_____
4. Questioning	_____	_____	_____
5. Genuineness	_____	_____	_____
6. Assertiveness	_____	_____	_____
7. Confrontation	_____	_____	_____
8. Problem Solving	_____	_____	_____

YOUR COMMENTS

   1. Significant behavior on your part or that of the person with whom you had the contact.

      _____

      _____

   2. Plans for the next contact.

      _____

      _____

   3. Things for you to do to assist in your growth.

      _____

      _____

                       Checked by _____
                                             Peer Helping Trainer

*This sheet may be duplicated so as to have several copies available.

STRATEGY DEVELOPMENT
SD 2

ASSISTING OTHERS
THROUGH
CONFLICT MEDIATION

CONFLICT MEDIATION

The following activities provide strategy for enabling peer helpers to apply their skills in assisting others as they resolve their conflict through mediation. This implementation Strategy permits immediate opportunity for peer helpers to utilize new skills and to be of assistance to self and others. Activities in this module are an introduction to various strategies for peer helpers.

From fighting and name calling on the playground to stabbing in halls, to the shootings in schools, to the street gangs that threaten the neighborhoods, to the inability of business to negotiate a fair deal, to unions fighting management, and to nations fighting other nations, conflict seems to be the current theme. The end result on the one hand is fear in some and power-seeking by others.

As our society has become more complex, and as people have a difficult time solving problems in a peaceful manner, they often lean toward conflict. From whole countries that go to war, to neighborhoods that riot, to gangs that use violence to solve problems, to individuals that choose to fight physically rather than talk it out, to the workplace where people have had to be tough to survive the conflicts, to the schools where youth are afraid, conflict mediation is a strategy to solving problems peacefully.

The days of "West Side Story," of wine, women, and song, have exploded into today's crime and music that seems to glorify conflicts and violence. Youths between the ages of 13 and 18 comprise about 11% of our population. Recently, this same age group was responsible for 41% of the arrests for offenses such as homicide, rape, robbery, aggressive assault, and burglary. One school that uses mediation has reduced fighting by 50% and office referrals by 75% (Ferguson-Florissant School District, St Louis County, 1991).

Skilled conflict mediators have been able to assist those in conflict, to resolve minor disagreements, to help with bigger problems of unions and management, to participate in gangs developing and dissolving, to helping neighborhoods living peacefully. Mediation is a skill that builds on the skills that you already have learned, that helps groups solve problems.

Mediation means a structured but informal process conducted by one or more third-party person(s) that operates totally without coercive powers. The agreement that is reached is designed by the parties themselves. The parties present the point of view, and the mediator working with the disputants actively assists them in designing an agreement that meets both sides needs. Participation is always voluntary.

```
┌─────────────────────────────────────────────────────────────┐
│                                                             │
│  MEDIATION IS                                               │
│                                                             │
│     •  a voluntary process.                                 │
│     •  non-adversarial.                                     │
│     •  using peer helpers who are impartial.                │
│     •  in a private setting.                                │
│     •  a process in which those in dispute listen to each   │
│        other, negotiate, and design a mutual agreement.     │
│                                                             │
└─────────────────────────────────────────────────────────────┘
```

```
┌─────────────────────────────────────────────────────────────┐
│                                                             │
│  A CONFLICT MEDIATOR                                        │
│                                                             │
│     •  listens to both sides carefully.                     │
│     •  asks questions.                                      │
│     •  empathizes with each party in a nonthreatening manner.│
│     •  can be assertive at times.                           │
│     •  does not take sides.                                 │
│     •  does not place blame.                                │
│     •  helps to think of options.                           │
│     •  does not force a solution on the disputants.         │
│     •  does help those in dispute decide on a resolution.   │
│                                                             │
└─────────────────────────────────────────────────────────────┘
```

You need, of course, to attend to those in conflict. Through the art of using empathy and open-ended questions those in conflict are allowed to tell their story. At times, you may need to use genuineness skills so that they know you are real and at other times, you may need to use skills of Assertiveness and Confrontation to keep those in conflict focused on the problem. An understanding of personality type helps one reduce some of the tension around conflict. Skills you learn in problem solving become vital as you assist those in conflict to brainstorm solutions and come up with the best alternative. Effective management of conflict is an important and necessary tool for our fast paced society.

You will now become aware of how you deal currently with conflict and your feelings about conflict. You will understand how your personality type impacts, how you feel about conflict and your approach to coping with conflict. Next you will learn specific guidelines for resolving conflict and finally how to help you personally resolve the conflict. You will have an opportunity to role-play various situations where you might use these new skills as you prepare to become a mediator.

Exercise SD 2.1

Name _____

Date _____ Hour _____

HOW I HANDLE CONFLICT

Experts believe that participating in conflict takes a lot of emotional energy. If people avoid conflict, ultimately this effects them by causing them to have low self-esteem and feeling angry. If people are observing conflict, it takes its toll on them by causing rapid heart rate and becoming emotionally blunted. Certain personality types have more difficulty with conflict than others.

GOALS

In this exercise you will

1. assess your current ways of handling conflict.

2. identify ways that you can be a conflict mediator through using your peer helping skills.

DIRECTIONS

1. List situations in which you were involved in conflict.

   a. You were participant in a conflict (yelled at someone or hit them).

      _____

      _____

   b. You avoided a conflict.

      _____

      _____

   c. You observed a conflict (listened to people yell over how to spend money).

      _____

      _____

2. Identify your reactions.

   a. physically _____

      _____

b. verbally _____

_____

c. change in feeling _____

_____

3. Describe the outcome/result.

a. solved peacefully _____

_____

b. solved violently _____

_____

c. not resolved _____

_____

d. avoided _____

_____

e. other (specify) _____

_____

4. As you preceive yourself, identify (check) your conflict comfort level when you are around conflict?

_ a. Okay
Conflict Mediation will be a natural role for me

_ b. Neutral
With help I believe I will be able to serve as a mediator

_ c. Not Okay
I feel unsure, however, I want to complete this module and then reevaluate. If I still feel the same way, conflict mediation may not be an appropriate role for me.

HOMEWORK

1. Keep a notebook of opportunities that you have to participate or observe conflict in the next several weeks.

2. Review Exercise SD 2.2 before the next group meeting.

Exercise SD 2.2

Name _____

Date _____ Hour _____

IMAGING SELF IN CONFLICT

To be able to solve conflict peacefully, you must be able to imagine yourself problem solving.

GOAL

In this exercise you will utilize imagery to see yourself solving a conflict.

DIRECTIONS

1. Listen to your trainer take you through an imagery exercise to solve conflicts.

2. Draw a picture of yourself resolving a conflict.

SELF PORTRAIT—SELF SOLVING CONFLICT

3. Explain how it felt to be in conflict. _____

_____

_____

HOMEWORK

1. Throughout the next few weeks, imagine yourself at least once a day resolving a conflict.

2. Complete Exercise SD 2.3 before the next group meeting.

3. Each day this week, before going to sleep, practice using imagery and, if you make a tape of the relaxation activity, use the tape.

4. After a couple days of practicing, recall a conflict situation and try to utilize the relaxation and imagery work to solve it.

Exercise SD 2.3

Name _____

Date _____ Hour _____

CHANGING CONFLICT THOUGHTS INTO PEACEFUL THOUGHTS

GOAL

In this exercise you will learn that one of the keys to developing effective resolution skills is to think peacefully.

DIRECTIONS

1. Discuss with some others the difference between solving problems peacefully and in conflict. What did you find out?

_____

_____

_____

2. Think of times when you were in conflict, and answer the following:

a. What was the conflict? Describe it.

_____

_____

_____

b. What did you say to yourself (self talk)?
   Examples: "I can get them."
               "I know how to handle this."

_____

_____

_____

c. How did you behave? Describe.

_____

_____

_____

3. Think of a time when you solved a conflict peacefully, and answer the following:

a. What was the conflict? Describe it.

_____

_____

_____

b. What did you say to yourself (self talk)?
    Examples: "I can work this out."
                "I can understand why he/she feels that way."

_____

_____

_____

c. How did you behave? Describe.

_____

_____

_____

4. Discuss with others in your training group the answers to Directions 2 and 3, specifically the self talk.

HOMEWORK

1. During the next week, record those times that you experienced solving problems peacefully. Use the questions in Direction 3 as an outline for your record keeping on each situation.

2. Study Exercise SD 2.4 and complete what you can before the next group meeting.

THE 4 Ds

When you are in a potential conflict you must be able to do certain things to pull yourself out of the conflict.

GOAL

In this exercise you will learn a number of ways to avoid or stop conflicts.

DIRECTIONS

1. Study the four step conflict stoppers listed on the next page. Notice that the procedure for stopping conflicts is divided into four simple steps.

2. Discuss in your training group the meaning of each of the four steps.

3. The trainer will help you identify a conflict situation that has happened to you. Regroup into small groups of three persons each and then role-play your conflict.

    a. First practice it with another member of your group, one will be the person causing the conflict. The third member will observe and give feedback afterwards.

    b. Practice it using the four step conflict stoppers.

    c. Rotate so that each one of you in the group has an opportunity to role-play his/her conflict as written on the card.

4. Perform one of your role-plays in front of the group and discuss as directed by your trainer.

    a. What error did the person make that got them into the conflict situation?

    _____

    _____

CONFLICT STOPPERS — THE 4 Ds

developed by Judith A. Tindall, Ph.D. and Shirley Salmon, Ph.D.

1. DETECT

Learn to Spot Conflict

Decide to Get Involved

2. DETACH

Flash the Mental Stop Sign

Relax

Change Negative Thought to Positive

Send Positive Message to Self

3. DIFFUSE

Use Empathy

Give "I" Message

Say No

Give New Idea

4. DEPART

Leave the Scene

Go to a Trusted Person

b. How did the group handle the conflict?

_____

_____

c. What other ideas might have been helpful to resolve the conflicts?

_____

_____

5. Discuss as a group ways that you have learned to avoid conflict.

6. As a goal for yourself, write in the space below the steps that you would follow to avoid conflict. (Number your steps.)

_____

_____

_____

_____

_____

_____

HOMEWORK

1. Review Exercise SD 2.5 before next group meeting.

2. Try using the four Ds in your everyday life and later share your experiences with the group.

3. Write your responses to each of the four cases that follow. Be prepared to bring the homework back to the next group meeting.

CASE 1: Jim was standing in line waiting for the movies. Another student named Bill crowded in front and said "Get out of the way. This is my place and not yours." What should Jim do to avoid the conflict with Bill?

_____

_____

_____

_____

CASE 2: You are sitting next to Susie at work. She continues to smoke and you are allergic to smoke. It really bothers you that she chooses to smoke at work even though there are rules against it. What should you do to avoid conflict?

_____

_____

_____

_____

CASE 3: Jim and Ray were walking down the street. Jim turned to Ray and called him a name, then he started asking him to fight. He kept calling him all kinds of names. This made Ray very upset. What should Ray do to avoid the conflict?

_____

_____

_____

_____

CASE 4: Susie was very popular at work. She was liked by most of her coworkers. Someone began spreading rumors about her that were not true. Others started making fun of her. What should Susie do to avoid conflict?

_____

_____

_____

_____

Name _____

Date _____ Hour _____

USING PERSONALITY TYPE TO COPE WITH CONFLICT

Any conflict resolution approach that does not consider personality differences is doomed to fail. Knowledge of personality type can lead to a heightened awareness that affords those in conflict better coping skills and more accessible alternatives during a conflict.

GOAL

In this exercise you will learn how different personality types cope with conflict.

DIRECTIONS

1. Divide into two groups—Thinkers and Feelers. (Remember that this preference is how one makes decisions.)

    a. On newsprint or chalkboard, place answers to the following questions according to the personality type of your group— Thinker or Feeler.

    How do you define conflict?

    How do you handle conflict at home and at work/school?

    What would you like others to keep in mind when they are in conflict and you are around?

    b. Share the responses with the total group.

2. Divide into Extroverts and Introverts.

    a. On newsprint, place how each group likes to deal with conflict.

    b. Share with the total group.

3. Divide into Sensors and Intuitive. (Remember that this is how we gather information.)

    a. Look at a picture for one minute.

    b. Have each group record what they saw.

    c. Share with the total group.

4. Discuss how would different preferences deal with conflict.

    E _____

    _____

    I _____

    _____

S _____

_____

N _____

_____

T _____

_____

F _____

_____

J _____

_____

P _____

_____

5. Study the following suggestions for different preferences. Then try to remember these so that you can use these suggestions when in conflict.

PREFERENCES SUGGESTIONS FOR HANDLING CONFLICT	
Extraverts:	Stop and listen to others.
Introverts:	Say what you are thinking.
Sensors:	Keep in mind that conflicts have more than just facts.
Intuitive Types:	Stick to the presenting problem. Don't make problems bigger.
Thinkers:	Allow others to express emotion.
Feelers:	Be direct and assertive.
Judgers:	Keep in mind that others might be right.
Perceivers:	Take a stand.

6. How can you handle conflict differently with your knowledge of type?

_____

_____

7. How can you help others who are different than you manage conflict?

_____

_____

HOMEWORK

1. Review Exercise SD 2.6 before the next group meeting.

2. Be prepared to follow through on Directions for Exercise SD 2.6.

Exercise SD 2.6

HELPING OTHERS THROUGH PEER MEDIATION

You are now ready to help others resolve conflicts. The following are suggested steps in setting up a conflict mediation program in your location. This can be a formal process or an informal process.

GOAL

In this exercise you will role-play the process of conflict mediation.

DIRECTIONS

1. Review the steps in a formal conflict mediation process and then discuss in the group meeting. A copy of Steps and Skills Used in Conflict Mediation is provided later in this exercise.

2. Role-play the steps in conflict mediation using the following examples:

    a. Two high school boys fighting in the hall over the fact that one boy was trying to take another's girlfriend out.

    b. Two women at work are angry because one of them is doing more work than the other.

    c. One person is upset because a friend borrowed a shirt and has promised to give it back and has not.

    d. Make up your own examples of two people in conflict.

3. Get feedback on the role from the observer. Use the Observer Form provided in this exercise.

4. Work with your trainer to set up the conflict mediation program in your location.

MEDIATION PROCEDURES

A.   Rights of Those in Conflict
1.   People in conflict have an option
     a.   to be disciplined or
     b.   to be referred to mediation.
2.   If mediation is requested, they have the option of going directly to mediation or establishing a time to go in the near future.

B.   Requirements of People Requesting Mediation
The people must agree to the following guidelines:
1.   no name calling,
2.   listen to each person and the peer mediators, and
3.   be willing to go along with the solution.

C.   Processing Request for Mediation
1.   Teachers or supervisors are given referral forms.
2.   The request for peer mediation is given to the peer helper professional.
3.   The peer helper professional decides who will work with the people in conflict. It is best to have two mediators.
4.   The two peer mediators and people in conflict go into a room and solve the conflict.

D.   Steps in Mediation Process and Skills Used
For the specifics, see the sheet entitled Steps and Skills Used in Conflict Mediation provided in this exercise.

E.   Evaluation
Do an evaluation with
1.   Professional Peer Helper and
2.   People with whom mediation was done.

F.   Review the Process
See the sheet entitled Review Process with Related Mediation Procedures Utilized for a format to follow in the review process.

HOMEWORK

1.   Read Strategy Development 3 following.

2.   Serve as a conflict mediator, fill out the contract, and come to the next group meeting to share experiences.

REVIEW PROCESS
WITH RELATED
MEDIATION PROCEDURES UTILIZED

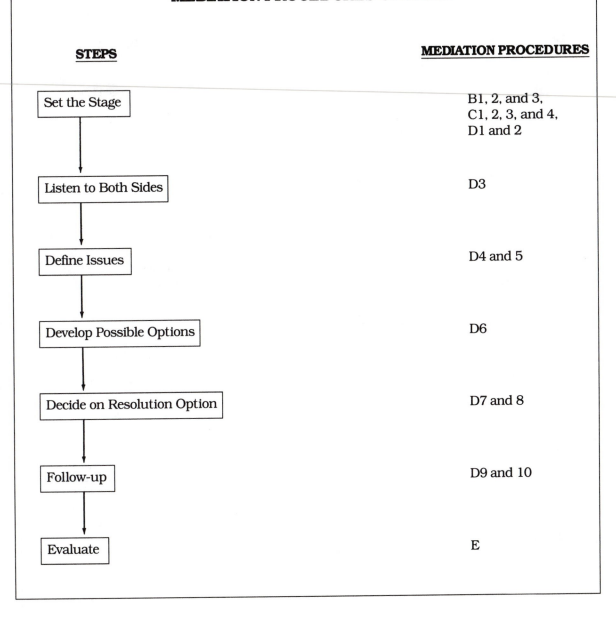

STEPS	MEDIATION PROCEDURES
Set the Stage	B1, 2, and 3, C1, 2, 3, and 4, D1 and 2
Listen to Both Sides	D3
Define Issues	D4 and 5
Develop Possible Options	D6
Decide on Resolution Option	D7 and 8
Follow-up	D9 and 10
Evaluate	E

STEPS AND SKILLS USED
IN CONFLICT MEDIATION

STEPS

SKILLS USED

1. Introduce self and welcome those to mediation

Genuineness
Assertiveness

Make an opening statement.

Example: "My name is _____ and my other peer mediator is _____. I will be your mediator today. I have been a peer helper for three months and have been trained as a peer mediator. I want to thank you both for coming. Remember, this is voluntary.

In order for us to get started I want to explain the steps we will go through. First, I want both of you to agree on some guidelines. Second, we want to listen to each of you tell your side of the story. During that time we may ask questions. Third, we will all think of several options to solve the conflict, and finally, we will come up with a resolution on which both of you can agree."

2. Present guidelines and get disputants to agree on the guidelines.

3. Listen to both sides.
    a. Listen to each person tell his/her story.
    b. Fill out contract as you get information.

Questions
Empathy
Confrontation
Attending
Summarize

4. Define issues.

5. Put in Type Information.

Type Framework

6. Brainstorm possible solutions.

Problem solving

7. Decide on resolution option.
    a. Ask each person which solutions he/she would use.
    b. Seek a common resolution.
    c. Have each person repeat in his/her words the resolution to which he/she agreed.

Problem solving

8. Have people sign contract. See a sample contract provided in this exercise.

Problem solving

9. Follow-up with the persons to determine whether or not the conflict has been resolved. If not, set up another meeting.

10. Remind them that they can return to mediation.

Name _____

Date _____ Hour _____

OBSERVER FORM*

A. Peer mediation observer form steps followed (add comments where appropriate).

DIRECTIONS

Write name of peer mediator(s) and check your concepts regarding steps used. Check H for high, M for medium, and L for low. Add comments where appropriate

Peer Mediator _____

H   M   L

__ __ __ 1. Introduction. _____

__ __ __ 2. Rules. _____

__ __ __ 3. Listening to story. _____

__ __ __ 4. Brainstorming. _____
            (Identify three solutions)

__ __ __ 5. Three solutions. Best solution. _____

__ __ __ 6. Contract signed. _____

B. Skills used

H   M   L

__ __ __   Attending _____

__ __ __   Empathy _____

__ __ __   Questioning _____

__ __ __   Genuineness _____

__ __ __   Assertiveness _____

__ __ __   Problem solving _____

__ __ __   Others (Specify) _____

__ __ __   _____

__ __ __   _____

__ __ __   _____

*This form may be reprodued for use in peer helping program

CONTRACT*

1. Names of people in conflict

   _____

   _____

2. Conflict summary.

   _____

   _____

3. Solutions. (List at least three.)

   _____

   _____

   _____

4. Solutions picked.

   _____

   _____

I agree to try this solution.

_____   _____
Name   Name

_____   _____
Date   Date

*This form may be reproduced for use in peer helping program.

STRATEGY DEVELOPMENT

SD 3

WHAT NEXT?

You have spent many hours learning core helping skills. Those hours have been exciting, and at times, probably painful. The thirteen modules concerning helping and the art of helping which you just completed were designed for you to understand what helping is all about. You now know well that helping is not simply giving advice. Skills you learned in "attending" already have paid off for you in that you listen, attend to what others are saying. Probably your friends and family believe that you are much more interested in them and as a result you probably have more people attending to you.

As a result of your skills in avoiding "communication stoppers," you will have people opening up to you more and giving you more cooperation. The invaluable skill of learning empathy enables you to really tune in to what others are saying. By your knowledge of how to be an effective listener, you have opened doors for people in helping them feel that someone cares. By your accurate feedback to people, you are able to help them make decisions that reflect their thoughts and feelings.

As you learned the skills of effective questioning, you probably noticed that people now are more able to be open with you and not become as defensive.

You now have the skills for effective listening and this puts you into the role of a good listener. Effective listening begins with your ability to enter into another person's frame of reference—to understand and appreciate the uniqueness of each person's experience and to use this experience to affirm a person's human potential. To help this person develop has required you to utilize the skills of truly "hearing" what others are saying, acknowledging your understanding by providing meaningful responses. These interpersonal skills are the first building blocks for increasing one's effectiveness as a helper.

Your skills will help you in listening to friends and family members when they are experiencing problems. You also will be able to respond to people needing help with various aspects of their lives, helping a new person in your school, work site, organization, or neighborhood. Feel proud of your skills because these are now a part of you and will help you throughout your life.

You have learned additional skills that will help you be more open, assertive, and confronting when you are worried about someone else or when someone is bothering you. For example, by using skills you have learned in this introductory peer helper training program you no longer will hold back when a friend does something to you that bothers you and you will not let salespeople push products on you that you do not want. If in the past you were frustrated by working for a boss to whom you couldn't stand up, now is the time to apply your new skills in a helpful manner so that you and your boss are more open, honest, and communicative with each other.

If you are part of trying to resolve conflict, these skills will be helpful.

As you apply your peer helper skills, you may realize the need for additional knowledge and skills. For example, if you are concerned about a family member or friend that has a problem with drugs or alcohol or other problems and you don't know what to do, then learning intervention skills will assist you in confrontation and helping the person and/or situation.

Personal development and growth are important skills for an effective helper. Often we miss growing to our fullest potential by not understanding our strengths and values. By understanding our own strengths, this enables us to have the fuel to move through difficult situations. *Peer Power, Book 2, Workbook: Applying Peer Helper Skills* was designed to assist you in developing these strengths and learning other skills.

As helpers we are often faced with others experiencing stress and leading a very unhealthy life-style. We also are faced with people involved with drugs and alcohol. Before you can help others with these problems, you must become aware of your own stress and your own attitudes and values concerning alcohol and drug use and abuse and be able to manage your own life effectively.

Often with these highly developed human-relations skills, you will be called upon to move into a leadership position where you will need skills for leading discussions, organizing your time, and setting priorities. A helpful next step for you as a potential leader is to learn skills that will make that job easier.

We encourage you not to stop with the completion of *Peer Power, Book 1, Workbook,* but instead to continue your training so as to learn additional skills. As you do, you will be able to expand your area of peer helping as you become knowledgeable about drugs and alcohol, wellness, your own potential, and leadership skills.

You now have the foundation; by continuing your training you will be able to build the total building. You are a model; others will follow you. Therefore, gain additional skills so as to apply better the peer helping techniques you have learned. Good luck with your peer helping in action. Your *Peer Power, Book 2, Workbook: Applying Peer Helper Skills* contains modules and exercises to assist you in your continued development as a peer helper.

"A Loving Person Lives in a Loving World"

"A Hostile Person Lives in a Hostile World"

"Everyone You Meet is Your Mirror"

ADDITIONAL READINGS

Alberti, R.E., & Emmons, M.L. (1974). *Your perfect right: A guide to assertive behavior.* San Luis Obispo, CA: Impact.

Benfar, R. (1991). *Understanding your management style.* Lexington Book, Lexington, MA.

Carkhuff, R.R. (1969). *Helping and human relations* (Vol. 1). New York: Holt, Rinehart, and Winston.

Carkhuff, R.R. (1972). *The art of helping.* Amherst, ME: Human Resource Development Press.

Egan, G. (1975). *The skilled helper.* Monterey, CA: Brooks/Cole.

Foster, E.S. (1992). *Tutoring: Learning by helping.* Minneapolis, MN: Educational Media.

Frey, D., & Carlock, C.J. (1989). *Enhancing self esteem, second edition.* Muncie, IN: Accelerated Development.

Gazda, George, et al. (1973). *Human relations development.* Boston: Allyn & Bacon.

Gordon, T. (1977). *Leader effectiveness training.* New York: Bantam Books.

Harris, T. (1967). *I'm O.K., you're O.K.* New York: Avon Books.

Hendricks, G., & Roberts, T. (1977). *The second centering book.* Englewood Cliffs, NJ: Prentice-Hall.

Hodgkinson, H. *"Guess Who's Coming to Work"* (1992). Northwest Regional Education Laboratory, Education & Work Conference, 1990. Institute for Educational Leadership.

Hodgkinson, H. *"Drug demographics: A look at the future,"* 8th Annual DASA Prevention Conference, March 1992. Lisle, IL.

Hoper, C., Kutzleb, U., Stobbe, A., & Weber, B. (1975). *Awareness games.* New York: St. Martin's Press.

Isachen, O., Berens, L. (1991). *Working Together.* Coronal, CA: Neworld Management Press.

James, M., & Jongeward, D. (1971). *Born to win: Transactional analysis with Gestalt experiments.* Reading, MA: Addison-Wesley.

Johnson, D. (1972). *Reaching out.* Englewood Cliffs, NJ: Prentice-Hall.

Kehayan, V.A. (1992). *Partners for change.* Rolling Hills Estates, CA. Jalmar Press.

Keirsey, D., & Bates, M. (1984). *Please understand me.* Del Mar, CA: Prometheus Nemesis.

Kroeger, O., & Thuesen, J. (1992). *Type Talk at Work.* New York, NY: Deiacorte Press.

Myers, (1980). *Gifts differing.* Palo Alto, CA: Consulting Psychology Press.

Myrick, R.D., & Bowman, R.P. (1973). *Peer helpers and the learning process.* Elementary School Guidance and Counseling, 18, 111-7.

Myrick, R.D., & Bowman, R.P. (1981). *Becoming a friendly helper: A Handbook for student facilitators.* Minneapolis, MN: Educational Media.

Myrick, R., & Folk, B. (1991). *Training peer facilitators for prevention education.* Minneapolis, MN: Educational Media.

Phelps, S., & Austin, N. (1975). *The assertive woman.* San Luis Obispo, CA: Impact.

Provost, J, (1990). *Work, play and type: Achieving balance in your life.* Palo, Alto, CA: Consulting Psychology Press.

Rogers, C.H. (1980). *A way of being.* Boston: Houghton Mifflin.

Samuels, D., & Samuels, M. (1975). *The complete handbook of peer counseling.* Miami, FL: Fiesta Publishing.

Satir, V. (1976). *Making contact.* Millbrae, CA: Celestial Arts.

Saunders, F.W. (1991). *Katharine & Isabel: Mother's light, daughter journey.* Palto, Alto CA: Consulting Psychology Press.

Sears, P.C., & Sherman, V.S. (1964). *In pursuit of self esteem.* Belmont, CA: Wadsworth.

Simon, S. (1973). *I am lovable and capable (IALAC).* Allen, TX: Argus Communications.

Simon, S., Howe, L., & Kirschenbaum, H. (1972). *Values clarification: A handbook of practical strategies for teachers and students.* Williston, VT: Hart Publishing.

Sue, D.W., & Sue, D. (1980) *Counseling the culturally different: Theory & practice.* New York: Wiley.

Varenhorst, B.B. (1980). *Curriculum guide to student peer counseling training.* Portola Valley, CA:

Varenhorst, B.B. (1983). *Real friends: Becoming the friend you would like to have.* New York: Harper.

ABOUT THE AUTHOR

JUDY TINDALL, Ph.D., has been a psychologist, counselor, and consultant since 1965. She is presently a psychologist and L.P.C. with Rohen and Associates Psychological Center. She currently is an associate professor for Lindenwood College. She has worked 18 years in public schools as a counselor and guidance director.

She has held local, state, and national office in professional associations such as St. Louis Association of Counseling and Development, Missouri Association of Counseling and Development, American Association of Counseling and Development, and American School Counselors Association. She was responsible for the development of American School Counselors Association's first leadership conference. She has received outstanding Professional Service Awards from both St. Louis ACD and Missouri ACD. She currently serves on the Missouri Committee of Professional Counselors. She has served on the Board of Directors for the National Peer Helpers Association in which she serves as vice president. She is a member of American Psychological Association, Missouri Psychological Association, St. Louis Psychologist Association, Association for Psychological Types, ACA, MCA, the St. Louis Association for Training and Development, and Phi Delta Kappa. She is past president of Missouri Peer Helpers Association.

Dr. Tindall has written numerous articles concerning communication skills, effective guidance practices, substance abuse, stress management, wellness, team building, leadership training, eating disorders, and taking care of you. She has edited journals on Peer Helping.

She has consulted and done workshops with schools, church groups, hospitals and businesses such as McDonnell Douglas, Ralston Purina, Maritz, State of Georgia, Delivery Network, Monsanto, M.C.I., Western Union, St. Louis County Sheriff Department, Trans World Airlines, Metropolitan Sewer District, and A.S.T.D. Topics included a wide range of topics from Wellness, Stress Management, Time Management, Drugs and Alcohol, Hypnotherapy, Mid-Life Crisis, Peer Helping, Communication Skills Training, Career Education, Leadership Development, Team Building, Eating Disorders, Care of the Care Giver, and Sexism.

She received her Ph.D. in psychology from St. Louis University; a Specialist in Counseling and Psychology from Southern Illinois University, Edwardsville; a Master's Degree from the University of Missouri at Columbia; and a B.S. Degree in Speech and Political Science from Southwest Missouri State University. Dr. Tindall is married and lives with her husband and sons in St. Louis County. She enjoys playing golf and writing for leisure activities.